Hamster
Handbook

Patricia Bartlett

With Full-color Photographs
Drawings by Michele Earle-Bridges

BARRON'S

Acknowledgments

There are many people who deserve my sincere thanks for this book. First of all is my husband, Dick, who shared my enthusiasm for these creatures and who soon found we owned some 70 of them; Linda Price, of AAA Hamstery, who bred the prettiest Campbell's I've ever seen; Leroy Coffman, DVM; Lorraine Hill; Mike Slade, DVM; Thomas Keefe, DVM; Alice Clarke and Pam Krause of the Aquarium Connection, who provided me with my Roborovski's hamster; Jackie and Charlotte Hornsby of Pet Kingdom; and Pat Hunter, who has kept me both grammatically correct and coherent.

© Copyright 2003 by Barron's Educational Series, Inc.

All inquiries should be addressed to:
Barron's Educational Series, Inc.
250 Wireless Boulevard
Hauppauge, New York 11788
http://www.barronseduc.com

ISBN-13: 978-0-7641-2294-1
ISBN-10: 0-7641-2294-0

Library of Congress Catalog Card No. 2002043788

Library of Congress Cataloging-in-Publication Data
Bartlett, Patricia Pope, 1949–
    The hamster handbook / Patricia Bartlett.
        p. cm.
    Includes bibliographical references (p.).
    ISBN 0-7641-2294-0 (alk. paper)
        1. Hamsters as pets. I. Title.

SF459.H3B38 2003
636.9'356—dc21   2002043788

Printed in China
9 8 7 6 5

About the Author

Patricia Bartlett is an author who writes about historical and natural history topics. Before turning to writing, she worked as a museum director, a book editor, a college alumni coordinator, and as an ad agency rep and magazine production manager. She has written for web sites, trade publications, newspapers, and popular magazines. She has authored or coauthored more than 30 books on history or natural history.

Cover Photos

All cover photos by Zig Leszczynski.

Photo Credits

Gerry Bucsis and Barbara Somerville: pages 34, 38 (top right), 40, 46 (top and bottom), 51, 53, 54, 55 (top), 72, 90 (top), 119 (bottom), 134, 135 (top right, middle right, bottom right); Jim Harding: pages 75, 83; Lorraine Hill: pages 22 (top left and right), 55 (bottom), 71, 76, 77, 79 (bottom), 82 (bottom), 88, 89, 90 (bottom), 92 (top), 131, 132, 137 (all 3); Quality Cage Co.: pages 43, 49; all others by R. D. or Patricia Bartlett.

Contents

Preface

Long ago, in a land far, far away...

Actually, the long ago equates to somewhat more than half a century, and the far-away land was my boyhood home in western Massachusetts. As I sit typing in my north central Florida office, the Connecticut River valley is pretty much a faraway land. But a little hamster, rearranging the bedding in her cage next to my desk, brings back some memories.

Even as a lad I was enamored of all manner of animals, and fortunately, my parents indulged my interests. The nightly reading of the "Pets for Sale" ads in the local newspaper was pretty much a daily ritual. One night, while reading the usual ads for dogs and cats, I recall my father stopping and asking, "What's a hamster?" I was all of 10 years old and certainly had no idea. My father read the ad to me: "Syrian Golden hamsters, $10 each," and then added a phone number. "Let's call," he said.

So we did and were told that a golden hamster was like a little teddy bear. My father asked the seller if he'd take anything less than $10. After all, $10 was a lot of money in 1948. After a little dickering, a price of $16 for a pair was agreed upon, and we went to see what a golden hamster really was.

The seller was across town, so of course we tried to figure out in advance what we were going to see. I guess we came up with something, but it certainly wasn't at all like the little creatures we ultimately saw.

When we arrived, the seller took us down into his cellar, and there in a half a dozen 10-gallon terrariums were a couple dozen baby golden hamsters. Although they didn't look much like bears to me it was love at first sight. I knew that my allowance—both saved and for the foreseeable future—was going to be spent that day. And when we left, half an hour later, we had a cardboard box that contained a pair of baby golden hamsters.

That pair of hamsters thrived and bred like rodents. Only a matter of weeks after I got them, they had bred and produced their first litter of

The golden Syrian hamster was the first pet hamster.

But I do remember that from nearly complete obscurity, Syrian golden hamsters became a veritable pet rage. The little critters were in every pet store, as well as in the pet sections of five-and-dime stores. I thought it phenomenal that a little rodent—a member of a group not particularly liked by people—could become so popular.

A dozen years later, golden hamsters had not lost their allure as pets. I was managing a pet distribution company in central Florida, and our hamster sales stood at about 2,000 of the animals weekly. This was when hamsters of "odd" colors were making their debut. We were able to offer a fair percentage of banded hamsters, which were snapped up by our customers.

I still find hamsters among the most endearing of rodents, and as they wander from place to place, cheek pouches full to overflowing with seeds and fruits, they remind me of Mr. Magoo, the bubbling comic strip character who always seems to come out on top. How could one not fall for such an enchanting creature?

Dick Bartlett

babies. A few weeks later those babies begat babies of their own, and soon all my neighborhood friends had baby hamsters. We put our own ads in the paper and were able to sell a few—but only at reduced prices. Some went to pet stores, some to other breeders. Eventually all I had left was my original pair. And after a time they were too old to breed. Although I can't remember for certain, I imagine that my entire family breathed a sigh of relief.

Introduction

Acquiring a hamster may be part of a purposeful act, or it may just "happen." For many people, owning a hamster is part of being a parent. One way or another, either through your children's friends, a neighbor, or a school project, a cage with a hamster appears on the kitchen table, rather like a conjuror's trick. You regard the cage with faint surprise and a little bit of suspicion. "Was I part of this decision?" you ask, although no one answers. "Was I awake at the time?" There's still no answer, nor do you expect one. You already know that hamsters are legendary for their prowess in reproduction, and you're not fooled for a moment that the hamster in the cage before you has been in solitary confinement all his life, even if your child assures you he's a male. You rather expect to wake up early some morning to your kid's delighted squeal, "Fred had babies! Look!" What you may not expect is a litter size of 12.

This book is designed to take some of the work out of hamster keeping and to put in a bit of fun. Hamsters are far more than short-tailed mice wannabes. Hamsters are actually a group of about two dozen related species, all lumped together under the term hamster, as all dogs are lumped into the dog group. Some types have a well-developed social environment, living cheerfully together in underground warrens they excavate themselves and even tolerate other species moving in. Others want absolute solitude except for brief sexual contacts.

Hamsters are by nature wanderers. If necessary, the Syrian hamster (once called the golden hamster), the most common pet type, may travel far from its burrow each night in search of food. As it travels the hamster will shove seeds and other bits of vegetation into his capacious cheek pouches before trotting back home to empty the pouches. Well loaded, a golden hamster has a rotund look. Once back in its sleeping area, it will use its front feet to help empty the pouches, shoving busily from behind with much the same distracted "I'm late!" attitude of the March hare, before heading out again. Whether a hamster is from the wild or from the Bronx, once dawn breaks over the horizon,

Campbell's hamsters are one of the social hamster species and the second most-popular hamster.

it's bedtime and the hamster is horizontal and gently snoozing as you back out of your driveway (no, this doesn't seem fair to me, either).

The dining habits of hamsters have pretty much made them the enemy of farmers in their native homelands. They can become extremely numerous over part of their range. (A gestation period of 16–20 days and a litter size of 4–14 young play a role in this. You can imagine the number of male hamsters who've said, "What? AGAIN???") Working quietly at night, hamsters mow down swathes of wheat, oats, or other grain crops, neatly severing the stems at the ground and then nipping the stems into portable or pouchable lengths. The communal types may stash away up to 240 pounds (90 kgs) of grains, grasses, legumes, insect larvae, and potatoes in their burrows, which makes them Silas Marner runner-ups for hoarding. You can understand why a farmer wouldn't welcome their presence. Provide a small area for hoarding in your hamster's cage; as long as it doesn't tuck away food items that will spoil—or as long as you take those bits out—it will seem more secure. It *is* a good idea to save for the future, is it not?

Hamsters are nocturnal beasts, which means they won't miss you a bit during the day. When you get home in the evening, they'll awaken at their own speed and get ready for a bit of socialization. Unlike rats or mice, hamsters have no detectable body odor—at least, not detectable to us, which makes holding one, playing with one, pretending you've lost one as it scurries between your bed sheets, or offering your new pet a sunflower seed treat, more enjoyable. Because their urine is far less pungent than that of other rodents, cage cleaning is less onerous. Once a week is fine; once every two weeks will work. With an adult weight of 4–6 ounces (113–168 g), keeping your hamster well fed won't be an expensive proposition; each eats between one to two tablespoons of feed a day, every day.

So go back and look at that cage again. You and your pet are going to get along just fine.

Chapter One

The Hamster's Past

The laurel wreath for hamsters as pets can be proudly claimed by three men—Saul Adler, an English parasitologist, Israel Aharoni, a zoologist from the University of Jerusalem; and Albert Marsh, a highway engineer from Mobile, Alabama.

All of these men recognized the pet potential of the Syrian or golden hamster. Saul Alder gets the credit for realizing there *had* to be hamsters from the wild he could use in his research and for sharing those hamsters once he got them. Aharoni gets the credit for his dogged determination to literally dig out those first hamsters and, with the help of his wife, for raising the young hamsters. Marsh gets the credit for starting a hamstery, and for quite probably starting one of the first, if not *the* first, "make money by raising these animals at home" operations.

Early Recognition

Let's start at the beginning, and for the beginning of the hamster we need to go to the 1700s, because like everything else, history has a way of creeping into any discussion you have about any animal. For all of us, the domesticated hamster begins with the Syrian or golden hamster, *Mesocricetus auratus.* ("Almost like but not quite Cricetus" [another kind of hamster] and "golden," for their golden brown color.)

The Russells

The earliest published description or reference to the Syrian golden hamster was in the second edition of a book entitled *The Natural History of Aleppo.* In 1740 an English physician named Alexander Russell was practicing medicine in Aleppo, Syria, a country that in those days was beyond the ends of the earth. (In case you've forgotten, the republic of Syria lies along the easternmost end of the Mediterranean Sea, just west of the island of Cyprus and south of Turkey.)

Alexander Russell practiced in Syria for ten years, and during that time became an expert on the plague (there are no indications anywhere that he knew of the correlation between rodents and the

The golden hamster has been bred in captivity for more than 70 years.

spread of the plague; even something as basic as asepsis, or cleanliness, wouldn't be proposed until 1865).

In keeping with what a learned man would do in a new land, Alexander Russell took notes on the people, local flora and fauna, and the plague. He put together a book and called it *The Natural History of Aleppo,* which he published in 1756, after he had left Syria.

His younger brother, Patrick Russell, lived in Aleppo from 1750 to 1781. He made further notes and published the second edition of the natural history in 1797, after the death of his elder brother. (Both editions are long out of print. Once in a while, the first edition, the hamster-less one, is available from used book dealers, for about $1,600. The second edition has been reprinted, and used copies of the reprint run about $160. Yes, I'm tempted, and I hope you will be too.)

It is in the second edition that the golden hamster first appeared. Alexander may have known about the animal, but it was Patrick who first published the account. Patrick Russell wasn't all that wordy, I'll admit; his account is limited to a paragraph that described the number of French beans the animal had stuffed in parallel rows into the cheek pouches. Obviously, he was working with a hamster corpse. Russell commented about the green beans: "When they were laid loosely on the table, they formed a heap three times the bulk of the animal's body." That must have been one very hungry hamster, prior to its demise!

Patrick Russell thought the animal was essentially the same animal as the European hamster and referenced it *Mus Cricetus*, or the golden mouse. He did not record what he did with that animal.

And there the hamster rested, until 1839. That year, George Waterhouse, the curator of the London Zoological Society, made a presentation at a meeting of the Society, and described a new species of hamster. He based his description of *Cricetus auretus* on the preserved skin and skull from a single specimen the Society had received from Aleppo. The collector of the animal was unknown, but it would be hard to point the finger at anyone other than Patrick Russell. Some years later the genus was changed to *Mesocricetus*.

You'd think that the announcement of a new species of hamsters

Saul Adler's difficulty in obtaining the Chinese hamster led to the capture of the Syrian hamster.

would have excited someone—after all, they didn't even have electricity or light bulbs back in 1839—but indeed, the Syrian hamster, having had its brief brush with fame, sank again into obscurity until the late 1920s or perhaps even early 1930.

Saul Adler

Enter Saul Adler. Adler was a parasitologist at the Hebrew University of Jerusalem. He was studying the parasite that causes leishmaniasis. Also called kala azar, this is one disease you never want to get. It is spread by the bite of a fly and causes fever, anemia, and enlargement of the spleen, liver, and lymph nodes. It is usually fatal if not treated. The Chinese hamster (*Cricetulus griseus*) had proven to be a good study animal for the disease, but Adler was running into a wall. He was unable to breed enough for his research, not knowing about the importance of long days and short days (see page 28), and

shipments from China were unreliable. (China, as a country, had bigger fish to fry, so to speak. A new national government had come into power in 1929, only to be smacked with two widespread rebellions. The country was also in the middle of a famine that had killed some three million people.)

The Syrian or golden hamster that Patrick Russell described was much like today's Syrian hamster.

Adler wanted to use a hamster species that was endemic to the Middle East and would be easier to obtain than the Chinese hamsters. He may have known of the Syrian hamster described by Waterhouse, or perhaps he was hoping to acquire *Cricetus migratorius*, the Armenian hamster. He asked a colleague who was frequently in the field to find and bring back hamsters for his research. The colleague was Israel Aharoni.

Israel Aharoni

In addition to being a zoologist, Aharoni was a linguist, speaking and reading Arabic, Latin, Greek, Aramaic, and other European languages, as well as Hebrew. One of Aharoni's projects was to research the Hebrew names for the animals of the Holy Land, and as a result produce a record of what animals actually had inhabited the Holy Land. (A formal-looking photograph shows a pensive, solidly built man who looks as if he had a terrific sense of

One of the brighter color morphs of the Syrian is this honey satin.

humor.) Because Aharoni collected butterflies (he was a zoologist, remember?), he had become close friends with the local Turkish sultan who also collected butterflies. At that time, that part of the Middle East was under Turkish rule.

In 1930, Aharoni went into the field to look for hamsters for Adler.

Aharoni already knew about the existence of the Syrian hamster. When he got to the Aleppo area, he instructed his guide to entreat the local sheik for information about the location of what was then called the golden hamster. The sheik was amenable, and sent Aharoni and his crew to a cultivated field that indeed had a population of hamsters. The sheik even provided laborers to dig up the hamsters. From an excavation 8 feet (2.4 m) deep, the crew dug up a nest of a mother and 11 young.

The mother and litter were placed together in a box, and evidently the collectors stood over the box congratulating themselves and each other, because they saw what happened next. You probably know exactly what happened, because you know what a hamster does to her young if they are disturbed. The mother hamster killed the first pup that approached her after they were placed in the box.

The collectors were shocked and the mother was peremptorily plunged into a bottle of cyanide (that fixed her!). Aharoni and his wife took on the task of raising the remaining 10 pups. We don't know, of course, how old the pups were, only that their eyes were still closed. But Syrian babies nibble on solid food shortly after they first begin exploring out of the nest at 9–10 days, eyes still closed, so perhaps the task was not completely onerous.

Aharoni had great intentions, but admittedly he and his forbearing wife were neophytes at hamster raising. The pups were placed in a wooden cage (surely you can guess what happened next) and the growing hamsters soon figured how to gnaw their way out. They escaped twice from their caging and not all of them were recaptured (there's a lesson here for all of us).

Only four reached breeding age, and after an unfortunate mishap during a breeding effort, only three were left. Fortunately, both sexes were represented. A pair was placed in a hay-packed cage and the hamsters did exactly what they were supposed to do, which was mate and *not* kill each other.

Aharoni greeted the birth of that first litter as if they were the only hamsters in the universe. He threw in a little prophecy, which was so flowery one can't help but wonder if some libation was involved.

> "Only someone who has tasted true happiness, heavenly joy, can appreciate our elation over the fact that our efforts did not prove in vain... From now on there will be a species of hamster that will be fruitful and multiply even in captivity, and will be convenient for laboratory experimentation. How marvelous are thy works, O Lord!"

A Syrian female recaptures a wandering pup and returns it to the nest.

The offspring of that first union mated willingly, so willingly, in fact, that the colony numbered 150 within a year. (There's another lesson here.)

Alder was given his experimental animals from that first colony, and indeed published his work in 1931 using the Syrian hamsters. A generous man, he provided breeding stock to other laboratories, including England. (I can tell you now, because the statute of limitations has passed, that the British stock was brought in, literally in Adler's pockets.)

And as time went on, Adler continued his extraordinary work on leishmaniasis and evolution, and translated Darwin's *Origin of Species* into Hebrew. But he always took particular pride in his role in domesticating the Syrian hamster.

Adler's generosity helped bring Syrian hamsters to India and the United States.

Hamsters in the United States

Adler sent hamsters to a research facility in India before World War II. His contact there sent hamsters to the United States: to Case Western Reserve School of Medicine in Cleveland (Ohio), and the Rockefeller Foundation in New York. A dozen hamsters were sent to the Public Health Service in Carville, Louisiana.

Leprosy Research

The hamsters were sent to Carville for specialized research; Carville was the site of the only leprosarium in the United States. Leprosy was considered such a disfiguring, communicable, and incurable disease that those who contracted it were quarantined for life in leprosariums. Science seemed

to be unable to find a cure for leprosy because we couldn't find an animal other than humans that could contract the disease. Research opportunities were limited.

Thus, with the thought that maybe the Syrian hamsters could be that longed-for research animal, hamsters were sent to Carville. Alas, the hamsters were as resistant as all other animals to leprosy. It wasn't until the 1980s that we found out we could give leprosy to armadillos, but we'd already found ways to cure the disease in the 1940s, so all the armadillos that wander the South are safe.

Carville's hamsters arrived in July of 1938, and a year later, the laboratory's Dr. S. H. Black dutifully reported on breeding the Syrian hamster in the *Journal of Leprosy*. (I can't help but smile, thinking of how many Syrians they must have had at that time, as Syrians have a gestation period of about 16 days!)

Of course those first three institutions shared their hamsters with other labs. Hamsters were sent to a lab in Berkeley, California, the NIH labs, and Tumblebrook Farms in Massachusetts. At this point they were still the dreamed-for research animal. In all honesty, that viewpoint hasn't changed much.

Albert Marsh and the Pet Market

Enter Albert Marsh, of Mobile, Alabama. Marsh was a highway engineer, a bit of a visionary, and a bit of a carny. He won a Syrian hamster in a bet. Intrigued with the little animal, he acquired more and set up his own colony. He named his business the Gulf Hamstery and Marsh Enterprises and went to work promoting hamsters as pets.

Marsh had a flair for the business, and he certainly knew how to work hard. He sold hamsters to individuals. He sold to laboratories. He took out ads in farming journals and promised to buy every hamster the reader could produce ("$1 for females and 75 cents for males at weaning age," which was real money in 1948). He served as an intermediary, buying hamsters from breeders and having them drop-shipped directly to other customers. He wrote a book on raising and breeding hamsters, and published it himself. His photograph in the book shows him with hamster caging in the background. Hamsters are in each hand

and crawling out of the pockets of his gentleman's long-sleeved white shirt. By 1951, Marsh's book had sold so well it was in its sixth edition.

Marsh even found time to do a little political maneuvering. In 1948 hamsters could not be brought into the state of California, because they were considered "wild animals." Marsh, with the help of the governor of Alabama, got California to recognize hamsters as domestic animals, thereby opening a new market for his enterprise. (I can't help but wonder why the governor of Alabama would get involved with a rodent breeding operation, but maybe by then there were a lot of hamsters in Alabama.)

But as with any new product, the laws of supply and demand caught up with Marsh. Pet stores began to buy their hamsters from inexpensive local backyard breeders. Infectious enteritis—called "wet-tail" because

Long-haired Syrians require more grooming than the short-haired variety.

One of the first color morphs of the Syrian was the banded Syrian.

of the unending diarrhea—evidently wiped out a lot of lab colonies, discouraging hamster use; antibiotic use for lab animals or pets was still in the future.

Marsh's markets dried up and so did his hamstery. He moved to California, and died there. But thanks to his work and his ability to hustle, hamsters had found an unbeatable niche in the pet market, and the pet industry had helped solidify that niche by marketing caging, foods, and accessories.

Today, the numbers of hamsters bred and used for research far outnumber hobbyist breedings. Laboratories buy hamsters from big commercial breeding facilities with well-documented lineages and rigid breeding standards. In 2000 some 200,000 hamsters were used in research in the United States alone and 90 percent of those were Syrians. Only the rat and mouse are more popular as research animals, and rats and mice run a poor second and third to hamsters as a pet rodent.

But the saga of the Syrian hamster doesn't end with the 1930 imports.

Michael R. Murphy

In 1971 Michael R. Murphy, then a graduate student at Massachusetts Institute of Technology, went to Aleppo, Syria, for the express purpose of capturing wild Syrian hamsters, and bringing them back for comparative research; after all, up to that point every single Syrian hamster in the lab and pet markets was a descendant of that single pair from 1930. Murphy and his wife, Janet, captured and brought back a dozen hamsters, and in that process, the hamster's charm hit again. Murphy commented that after only three days of handling, the hamsters he captured were tame and gentle. Those hamsters bred within a month of being captured, and all eight litters were brought up to weaning (the lessons learned by Aharoni have not gone unrefined). Murphy added, with gentle understatement, that it looked as if Aharoni was right when he predicted the Syrian hamster would be a wonderful lab animal.

Murphy included a photo in his account, found in Siegel's book. It shows him in the field in Aleppo, gingerly holding aloft the first wild hamster captured in 40 years.

Murphy is, quite understandably, smiling.

Chapter Two

The Basic Hamster

The term "hamster" actually refers to about 24 species of small rodents, all from the Old World and all of whom like to hoard food. Hamsters are part of a subfamily of rodents that includes the cotton and wood rats, harvest mice, lemmings, voles, and gerbils. In this subfamily, there are species that climb agilely (harvest mice), species that are excellent swimmers (muskrats), and species that scamper quickly from place to place, usually under cover of darkness (gerbils). The hamsters stand out in the group as secretive burrowers and hoarders. If we could save money the way hamsters save food, we wouldn't have to worry about Social Security; we'd just open one of our personal storage rooms and take out a sack or two of money to last until next month.

Description

As a group, hamsters are chunky-bodied, thick-furred, short-tailed rodents with large cheek pouches. They have short limbs, and although there's no opposing thumb on the forefeet, hamsters are quite dexterous when it comes to manipulating food or cage doors. Their teeth have a gap, called the diastema, between the front incisors and the molars. This gap permits easy manipulation of food and bedding materials. Some rodents can close their lips behind the incisors, which is why muskrats can gnaw while underwater and naked mole rats can literally chew their way through dirt when digging.

Names

The name "hamster" is said to be derived from the Middle High German "hamastra," which means to store. Of the many kinds of hamsters, only about five are found in the pet market, and considering their ability to reproduce, this is actually quite enough.

The hamster that occupies the front and center seat in the pet market is the Syrian hamster, *Mesocricetus auratus,* the "big" hamster. There are bigger hamsters from Middle Europe and Russia, but they

	Syrian Hamster *Mescricetus auratus*	Campbell's Hamster *Phodophus campbelli*	Winter White Hamster *Phodophus sungorus*
Adult length	6–8 inches (15–20 cm)	3¼–4¾ inches (8–12 cm)	2¼–4 inches (6–10 cm)
Adult weight	5–7 ounces (140–200 g)	1½–2 ounces (40–60 g)	1½–2 ounces (40–60 g)
Adult food consumption	⅓–½ ounces (10–15 g) dry food/day	¼–½ ounce (7–15 g) dry food/day	¼–½ ounce (7–15 g) dry food/day
Adult water consumption	6 t (30 ml) per day	2½–3 t (12–15 ml) per day	2½–3 t (12–15 ml) per day

aren't in the pet market. Because it was the first pet hamster, the Syrian is the best known. When most people think of hamsters, it's the Syrian that comes to mind. Syrians are known by a variety of other names. The first common name was the golden hamster, because they were indeed a golden brown color on the top, and a pale, muddy gray on their

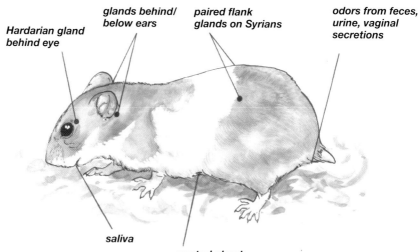

Hardarian gland behind eye

glands behind/ below ears

paired flank glands on Syrians

odors from feces, urine, vaginal secretions

saliva

ventral gland; if dwarf hamster

Hamster Scent Glands

Roborovski Hamster *Phodophus roborovski*	Chinese or Gray Hamster *Cricetus griseus*
1½–2 inches (4–5 cm)	4–5 inches (10–12 cm)
1–1½ ounces (25–40 g)	1½–1¾ ounces (40–50 g)
¼–⅖ ounce (7–12 g) dry food/day	¼–½ ounce (7–15 g) dry food/day
2–2½ t (10–12 ml) per day	2½–3 t (12–15 ml) per day

stomach. Some forms had an ashy stripe across the chest. Because golden hamsters have been selectively bred for different colors—one of which is indeed a light apricot gold—new descriptive names for these morphs have been coined. The previously "golden" hamster can be a banded brown and white, a light gold, black, or any of some 20-odd colors. Those bright eyes may be black, brown, or a shade of red, and the coat may be long or short. To keep things relatively simple, the golden hamster is now the Syrian hamster. There's even a hairless mutant Syrian called the alien hamster, but they aren't as readily available as the furred type, and not as appealing, either.

Common names are misleading, because you'll see the same names used for other hamster types. The teddy-bear hamster is one example. Some people use the term "teddy bear" for all long-haired Syrian hamsters. Others use it to describe the short-haired black Syrian hamster. In dwarf hamsters, the Djungarian—pronounced "Jung-gair-rian"—hamster is another confusing name. The term Djungarian is used for both the Campbell's and the winter white hamsters, because at one time we thought they were subspecies of the same animal. Even scientific researchers are a bit foggy on what a Djungarian hamster is (usually it's the Campbell's) and you'll find references to the Siberian hamster, yet another common name for the winter white hamster, as well (see page 19 for a more complete explanation). To keep things simple, if you want to buy a specific kind of hamster, just be certain you see the animal, or a photo of it, before you put your money down. People can be very indignant when you try to tell them that what they sold you isn't what they said it was.

Body Features

The Stomach

A hamster's diet is comprised largely of cellulose, which is hard to break down. This is why cows have more than one stomach and chew their food twice, and why termites carry protozoans in their guts. Kill the protozoans, and the termites die.

Hamsters digest their own food twice, and a two-compartmented

Hamsters carry seed in their cheek pouches.

Food nibbled by the hamster passes through the esophagus which is connected to the first stomach, near the narrowed portion that divides the stomach. The first part of the stomach (the forestomach) is nonglandular, meaning that stomach #1 plays a rather passive role in what happens to its contents, serving as sort of a holding bin for the action within. Bacteria in the first stomach begin the digestion process for their hamster host. The process is more fermentation than digestion, rather like what happens in the rumen of a cow. (You can already pick up on why antibiotics are deadly to hamsters. Antibiotics that destroy the friendly bacteria in the first stomach allow pathogenic bacteria to proliferate, and bam! No fermentation and the pathogenic bacteria churn out toxin, with deadly results.) But in this example, everything works just as it should and the semifermented food is sloshed through the stricture into stomach #2, the glandular stomach, in 10 to 60 minutes.

stomach is part of the arrangement. Hamsters are pregastric fermenters, just like the hippopotamus and the kangaroo. This term means that the food is allowed to soften a bit in the first stomach, via fermentation, before it's digested. Pregasteric fermenters are famous for their gastric capacity, another reason farmers hate the wild hamster, since hamsters can severely damage a farmer's grain crop.

The Pet Hamster Species

Class	Mammalia, all mammals
Order	Rodentia, all rodents
Family	Muridae, "mouselike ones," all mice, rats, gerbils, and hamsters
Subfamily	Cricetidae, "squeaking ones," all hamsters
Genera	Mesocricetus, "resembling but not quite like Cricetus," the European field hamster
	Phodophus, "blistered or tubercled foot"
	Cricetulus, "squeaking"

The long-haired Syrian is also known to some as the teddy-bear hamster.

The second "bin" of the stomach is geared up for action, with active digestive acids posed to further dismantle the food particles. Once the food particles are broken into absorbable components, they pass into the gut for absorption and extraction/absorption of water.

But the digestive process isn't complete. Hamsters consume part of their feces as the feces emerge from the anus, and by so doing are able to extract more nutrition, and a few extra vitamins, including vitamin K, from their food. The practice is called coprophagy, and hamsters do it up to 20 times a day. Animals that can survive in poor habitats, such as deserts, find ways to gain the most possible benefit out of what they eat and drink, and hamsters are no exception. This ability to wrest vitamin K, which assists in blood clotting, from the diet may be part of the reason that hamsters are naturally resistant to warfarin, which disables blood-clotting mechanisms and is used for rodent control.

The Syrian Hamster

Syrian hamsters are found from Romania and Bulgaria, southeastward to Asia Minor, the Caucasus, Israel, and part of Iran. They are burrowers, living on brushy slopes and steppes, where they dig their own burrows with the feet and teeth or find one to occupy. Burrows can be anywhere from 2 to 10 feet (61–305 cm) deep, usually with several entrances. The wild color is golden brown above, with a creamy white belly and chest. Some have a gray stripe across the chest.

Size: These are good-sized rodents, with a body length of 6–7 inches (12–17½ cm) and a tail about ½ inch (12 mm) long. Adults weigh between 5 and 7 ounces (140–200 g). Females are the larger sex. Because

Pet Trade Hamsters at a Glance

Species	Syrian	Roborovski	Campbell's	Winter White	Chinese
Size small 2.25–4 inches (6–10 cm)			X	X	X
Size large 4–7 inches (10–17 cm)	X	X			
Tail less the ⅓ head-body length	X	X	X	X	
Tail more than ⅓ body length					X
Color golden orange or variable	X				
Color gray or variable			X	X	
Color gray		X			X
Poorly defined or no middorsal stripe	X	X			
Well-defined middorsal stripe			X	X	X
Lateral/side stripe present				X	

Syrians are big, they are easier to handle. They seem to work well for children's pets because of their size, and they don't seem as nervous as the smaller or dwarf hamster types.

They respond well to gentle handling, and seem to enjoy it.

Hibernation: In the wild, Syrians can hibernate in response to cold and/or decreased food supply. Like

The Campbell's is also called the Djungarian hamster and the Russian hamster.

The normal Campbell's hamster, much as it looked in 1902 (but a 2003 version!).

marmots, they awaken periodically to eat, at which time they nibble on all that stored food. Researchers A. Terada and N. Ibuka found that older Syrians (20 months old!) start their hibernation earlier and spend more time in the sleeping mode than very young (three weeks at the start of hibernation) hamsters.

Families: Syrians generally live as individuals in the wild, although families—mother, father, and young—live together until the young reach sexual maturity. Like the European hamsters, each Syrian burrow has its own surrounding territory.

Food: These are the hamsters with the very large cheek pouches; a fully loaded Syrian looks a bit like an amused Mae West wearing an oversized fur collar. They venture out of their nests at night to find food and to load the cheek pouches. When the pouches are loaded, the hamster tends to sway a bit from side to side. Upon return to the burrow, they empty the pouches, using their front feet to help shove the food out from behind.

The cheek pouches for Syrians are rather like security blankets. An insecure Syrian may keep food in its pouches. A threatened Syrian may empty its cheek pouches if it thinks it may need to run.

Life span and breeding: Captive life span is two to two and one half years but some have lived as long as four years. In captivity, Syrians can have young every month of the year, although there is a marked decrease in fertility during the winter months,

Satin-coated Roborovski hamsters tend to look greasy— but it's the coat.

and after they are over a year and a half old (fertility is "greatly reduced," not "ended"). Litter size is usually 4–12 pups, after a gestation of 15–18 days. The pups have to share the 7–8 pairs of mammary glands.

The young begin nibbling at solid food when they're about ten days old, and are weaned at three weeks. They become sexually mature at 42 days for the males and 34 days for

All hamster types, like this Roborovski, practice coprophagy.

This bright, long-haired Syrian hamster weighs only about six ounces.

the females. Once beyond those dates of sexual maturity, Syrians need to be separated from each other. If they are different sexes, they'll fight and mate, or if they are the same sex they'll fight. Fighting is hard to ignore late at night, when the

Young Syrians begin nibbling solid food before their eyes open.

sounds of tussling and shrill squeaks will resound until you rise up from what had been a deep sleep and roar "Enough!," rather like Godzilla erupting indignantly out of the ocean after too many sonic wave tests. There is an easy temporary solution that involves no bloodshed; just put one of them in the bathtub until morning, but *do* close the drain.

Lines of inbred Syrian hamsters (20 or more successive generations of brother-sister pairings) are used for specialized research. The advantage of using inbred strains is that the individuals have the same genetic complement; those from a particular strain will have the same reaction when tested in research. Strains are identified by names such as LSH/SsLak. The first three letters identify the lab that developed the strain, in this case the London School of Hygiene.

The Campbell's Hamster

The second most popular hamster is the dwarf Campbell's Russian hamster, *Phodophus campbelli*. The Campbell's is named for W. C. Campbell, who discovered it in Mongolia in 1902. It is found in arid areas in central Asia, northern Russia, Mongolia, and northern China.

Appearance: The "wild" morph has a grayish upper body and a white belly, with a thin, dark middorsal stripe. The feet are short, broad, and hairy. When this species was observed in Manchuria in the late 1930s, it was living with pikas, and shared the pikas' burrows, paths, and tunnels, especially in the winter.

Food: Those observed in the wild dig escape and ventilation tunnels leading away from the burrow entrance. They eat grasshoppers and other insects for moisture as well as food value. They are efficient at concentrating their urine to conserve water.

Size and life span: These are smaller hamsters, weighing about 1 ounce (females) to 2 ounces (males), and measuring from 3¼–4¾ inches (8–11 cm) from nose to tail tip. Males are the larger sex. Because they are smaller than the Syrians, they are harder to hold. These are social hamsters, living quite happily together if introduced/put together while they are young. They live about a year and a half to two years in captivity, but some have lived four years.

Breeding: The females dig a special nesting chamber just before they give birth, and line it with dried grasses and sheep's wool. They bear their young after a gestation of 18–19 days, and like other hamsters, they tend to be reproducing machines. (In captivity, researcher Francis Ebling found that if Campbell's are placed on a long-day cycle of 16 hours of light and 8 hours of darkness, the females can give birth again in just 20 days.) Under normal captive conditions the usual time may be as little as 36 days. This means they can mate when the young are one day old. They have four pair of mammae.

Care of the young: Unlike other rodent species, the male Campbell's plays a substantial role in the survival of the young. We are only beginning to realize how important those family bonds can be. Jennifer Jones and Katherine Wynne-Edwards published their observations of the Campbell's,

A winter white hamster has furred feet and dark dorsal coloring in three scallops along its side.

Campbell's hamster babies owe their survival in part to care from both parents.

showing that the male parent participates in the birth and rearing of the young. He assists mechanically during delivery, licks and sniffs the young in the moments after the birth, and opens the pups' airways by clearing the nostrils. Males continue to contribute to pup survival through direct care of the young. He even hops into the nest when the mother is absent, as does an aunt to the young, if one is caged with the pair.

As a result of the presence of these adults, pups are very rarely left alone in the nest and so are not subjected to cooling, an important survival factor when the pups are too small to maintain their own body temperature. But the young mature rapidly and reach sexual maturity at four weeks.

Campbell's hamsters arrived in Britain as lab animals in 1964. They progressed from the lab to the pet store in the early 1970s and to the United States shortly thereafter. Selective breeding has altered their original gray-brown coloration and white belly to some 40 color and coat combinations,

Campbell's versus Winter Whites

The Campbell's hamster may be called the Djungarian or the Siberian hamster, but these names are also used for the winter white hamster, *Phodophus sungorus*. The confusion began when the Campbell's and the winter white were considered races or subspecies of *Phodophus sungorus*, so they shared common names as well as a generic designation. Microscopic inspection of gut flora has helped separate them; the differing numbers and kinds of bacteria indicate small but real differences in digestion processes. Observations of these two types in the wild have also helped split them into separate species. Although both the Campbell's and the winter whites are nocturnal, the Campbell's awaken earlier—before dark—and remain outside the burrow, above ground, more than twice as long as the winter whites. They mark their trail with scents, so finding their way back is not a problem. The scents come from the glands behind the ears, the lower abdomen, and from feces, urine, and (in females) vaginal secretions. They pause outside the entrance to their burrow and groom themselves, rubbing their paws over their ears and around the eyes and by rolling. This helps transfer the scent to the paws so a scent trail is easily left.

Because they are above ground longer, the female Campbell's can travel farther than the female winter whites, although they travel at the same speed. But the male Campbell's travel almost three times faster than the female Campbell's, and they cover a much larger territory over the same amount of time.

When compared to the winter whites, the prolonged activity of the Campbell's indicates that they need more effort and energy to live in their colder, drier, and more seasonal habitat than the winter whites. The extra effort required for survival may also be the reason that both Campbell's parents are involved in care of the young.

The Winter Whites

The third type of hamster is the dwarf winter white Russian hamster. The winter whites' scientific name is *Phodophus sungorus*. They are also called Siberian hamsters or the Djungarian hamsters, which is why you can't trust common names. They bear the dubious distinction of causing more allergic response in humans than any other pet hamster species.

The normal winter white has dark fur during the summer.

The winter white during the winter has much paler fur.

The pearl winter white is white all year long.

Winter whites are from the grassy steppes of eastern Kazakhstan and southwest Siberia. Like ermine and snowshoe hares, they change coat color with the seasons, being dark-furred during the summer and white-furred during the winter. They'll do the same in captivity, providing their caging is illuminated with natural light. Mine never became entirely white-furred, but they lost their black side stripe and their gray coats became whiter and paler as the winter solstice approached.

In the wild, the winter whites live together in the very broadest sense. Each female shares separate burrows with at least two male winter whites. Those males share burrows with at least two females. When the young are born, the male shares in caring for the young.

Size and color changes: These are small hamsters, not as rounded or as small as the Campbell's ham-ster. They measure up to 4 inches (10 cm) from snout to tail. During the summer, they are dark gray-brown with a white to gray belly. There's a black stripe down the back, and a black stripe on each side separates the gray from the white. As the days grow shorter and winter approaches, their gray coat is shed and replaced by a white coat, but the black dorsal stripe remains. Captive breeding has brought us two other color morphs. One is the sapphire, a blue-gray color with a dark dorsal stripe, white to cream belly, and dark eyes. The other is the pearl white, which has a white body, ticked with gray hairs, and a darker head. Neither of these color morphs change their coat color with the short-day cycle during the winter.

These are small hamsters, with a body length of about 2¼–4 inches (5.3–10 cm). The tail is about ⅓-inch long (7–11 mm), and is usually tucked into the fur so you don't see it. They have larger eyes than the Campbell's hamster, smaller ears, and slightly thicker fur. Like the Campbell's, they live a year and a half to two years in captivity.

Hibernation: Despite the fact that these hamsters come from very cold areas, they do not hibernate. Instead, they slip into a morning torpor for a few extra hours of sleep. Their metabolic rate does drop during this sleep, but not enough for it to be considered hibernation. Instead, the winter whites must survive on hoarded food and whatever they can gather from the frozen landscape. You'd think this sort of edge-existence would stress the animals, but the opposite is true. Researcher Staci Bilbo of Johns Hopkins Hospital in Baltimore and her colleagues have found that those hamsters under short-day regimens (winter days) had more major immune cells and recovered faster from fever than those on long-day cycles (summer days).

During the 1960s, the winter whites were used as lab animals in Czechoslovakia. Two pairs were brought to a lab in Germany and from there made their way to the pet market. Their social nature made their transition to pets easy. They live well in small groups or in family groupings, although all-male groups get along best if put together while they are young.

Breeding: When a pair mates, the 4–6 young are born after a gestation of 18–19 days—generally. Both the Campbell's and the winter white hamsters can put pregnancy on "pause" after the mothers have been fertilized by the males. The process is called *postimplantation diaphase,* and it means the female parent can delay the onset of pregnancy. One benefit of this delaying is that the pups that are currently being fed by the mother will weigh more when they are weaned. In effect, the mother can channel her energy toward the current set of pups instead of dividing that energy between the pups and the embryos growing in her womb. The only other mammal that can do this is the bat. The female can also "choose" not to become pregnant; if the male(s) associated with her is removed or killed after mating with her, she will not become pregnant.

Female winter whites can give birth to another litter just 24 days after the birth of the first. Young become sexually mature when only a month or so old.

Winter white pups.

Winter white pairs form monogamous bonds. Lesley Castro-William and Kathleen Matt found that when animals were paired for three weeks,

Getting Coated with Trouble

It all seemed so simple, in retrospect: European fashion designers, wanting to work with something a little different, a short-napped, fur, perhaps, were casting about for a fur to use in their fall 2001 designs. The eyes of Italian designer Alberta Ferretti lit on hamster pelts, and *molto bene* (to use the Italian term for "very good"), two fall designs were created. One was a skirt suit of patchwork hamster pelts, brown, black, and white. The other was a camel skin full-length coat, lined with brown pelts. (In my experience, only a mole's pelt is softer than a hamster's, but I really don't see there ever being any sort of market for actual moleskin anything.) The suit was priced at $6,320, the coat at $6,030. *Molto cattivo* (again, Italian for "very bad")! Animal lovers rose up, aghast, dragged in the British Humane Society, pointed out that dog and cat fur products can't be sold in the United States, and hamsters should not be treated any differently, and sent hissing e-mails and indignant letters. Nonetheless (or perhaps *because of* the furor and publicity), the 12 suits in a London shop all sold.

then separated, the males demonstrated body and behavior changes that are similar to human depression. The males ate more and gained weight. They were less active, spending more time in their sleeping area and less time exploring their cage. Their testes shrank.

Care of the young: Wynne-Edwards observed litters of both Campbell's and winter white hamsters, and found that unlike the Campbell's hamsters, the winter white fathers rarely spent time in the nest alone with the young, although the male winter white does contribute to the care of the young. The young winter whites grow faster than the Campbell's during the first week or so of birth, probably because the female parent raises the temperature of the nest about 2°F (4°C) higher than nonbreeding levels. (The mother's resting metabolic rate is higher when she is with her pups; this adaptation and the ability to not become pregnant are just two of the reasons researchers are finding the winter white hamsters worthy research subjects.) Young *sungorus,* more than any other kind of pet trade hamster, need access to drinking water or a water source like fresh apple beginning at eight days of age in order to avoid growth retardation.

The Roborovski Hamsters

Roborovski's hamsters, *Phodophus roborovski*, are from the deserts of western and eastern Mongolia, China, and Russia. They were discovered in 1894 by Lieutenant Roborovsky, but weren't described until 1903. They weren't kept as pets until after 1970. They were brought to the United Kingdom from the Netherlands in 1990.

Size, color, and behavior: These are small hamsters, with a body length of about 4 inches (10 cm), and with a slighter build than either the dwarf Campbell's or the dwarf Russian. They live in single-entrance burrows in flat, sandy areas. They awaken later than the other dwarf hamsters, being most active from 9–10 P.M. They are well adapted to living in cold temperatures, and like Campbell's can concentrate their urine. They are brown in color, and have no middorsal stripe. Life span in captivity is three to three and a half years, but some have lived as long as four years. They live well in pairs. These are fast-moving hamsters, quick to scurry out of the way when they feel you might actually open their cage. They are so slight in body you almost hate to grasp them because you're afraid something might break. They seem to be a bit more nervous about being petted, although they do tame well. One hamster breeder found her Roborovsky hamster would crawl into her hand when she opened the cage door, then lie in her hand while she petted it until it fell asleep.

Breeding: My pair was understandably nippy and agitated about being disturbed while they had

Roborovski hamsters are quick and curious about everything.

young. If the parents think they're being bothered too much, they kill and eat their young. Usual litter size is 3–5 young, and gestation is 20–22 days. Breeding and young usually occur during the long days, but in captivity the longer days created by artificial lighting means your Robs may breed more frequently.

Once they accept the fact that you're not going to slurp them up like furry gumdrops, they do settle down and will raise their young, if you leave the mother and litter alone for the first week or so. They live quite well in family groups.

The Chinese Hamster

The fifth hamster in the pet market is the Chinese hamster, *Cricetus griseus.* It is also called the Chinese rat-tailed hamster, the striped-backed

Hamster Species (all members of the subfamily Cricetidae)

Genus	Common Name	Genus, Species
Cricetus	European Field Hamster*	*Cricetus cricetus*
Cricetulus	Armenian (gray) hamster*	*Cricetulus migratorius*
	Ladak	*Cricetulus alticola*
	Chinese striped*	*Cricetulus barabensis*
	Mongolian	*Cricetulus curtatus*
	Lesser Longtailed	*Cricetulus longicaudatus*
	Greater Longtailed	*Cricetulus triton*
	Tibetan	*Cricetulus kamensis*
	Kazah	*Cricetulus eversmani*
	Chinese	*Cricetulus curtatus*
	Dark	*Cricetulus obscurus*
	False Gray	*Cricetulus pseudogriseus*
Mesocricetus	Syrian*	*Mesocricetus auratus*
	Romanian*	*Mesocricetus neutoni*
	Turkish*	*Mesocricetus brandti*
	Ciscauscasion	*Mesocricetus raddei*
Mystromys	South African	*Mystromys albicaudatus*
Phodophus	Campbell's*	*Phodophus campbelli*
	Winter whites*	*Phodophus sungorus*

*used in medical research

hamster, the striped hamster, or the gray hamster, and comes from northern China and Mongolia. This is that very hamster that Saul Adler despaired of acquiring and so asked Israel Aharoni to find another hamster that could replace *griseus* in Adler's studies.

These hamsters are poorly adapted to extreme cold. They are found in rocky terrain and they are good climbers. Their burrows are often shallow, perhaps because it's hard to dig a deep burrow in rocky areas, but where space permits can be up to 3 feet (91 cm) deep, with

Research Use

Carcinogenesis

Cytogenetics and oncology

Cytogenetics, diabetes, toxicology

The sleek Chinese hamster has a dark dorsal stripe characteristic of many hamster species.

Hibernation, socialization, reproduction
Cytogenetics and taxonomy

Hibernation, taxonomy, cytogenetics

Cytogenetics, carcinogenesis, diabetes, obesity, photoperiod changes, social behavior
Cytogenetics, carcinogenesis, diabetes, obesity, photoperiod changes, social behavior

sleeping and food chambers branching off from the main tunnel, and may have two entrances. During spring and summer, all members of this genus are active day and night, but become more nocturnal as the days shorten. Although they do not hibernate, they do sleep longer during the short-day cycle. If discovered, they either freeze in place or run.

Size and description: These are small, slight hamsters, dark gray in color with a darker dorsal stripe. The belly is ivory to gray. Females have four pairs of mammaries. Body length is about 4–5 inches (10–13 cm), and their weight is about an ounce (43 g). Compared to the Syrians these are slight hamsters indeed. They carry their long, slender bodies on very short, slender legs. The tail is about twice the length as that of the Campbell's or the Syrian hamsters, which means it's all of 1 inch (25 mm) long. There are reports that it uses its tail to help balance itself when scurrying around on rocks. Its cheek pouches are very large.

Research animals: These hamsters were used as research animals at the Peking Union Medical College in 1919. In 1948 ten males and ten females were exported from China to the United States, to be used as beginning stock for a lab colony. Captive breeding was not successful until the researchers began to provide short-day and long-day cycles.

Once the techniques of captive breeding had been mastered, there were Chinese hamsters a-plenty, and they made the short hop to the pet market. It is also the only hamster species that cannot be legally kept in all 50 states. Before you take your Chinese hamsters over state lines, especially into California, check with the game and fish commission or the Department of Agriculture of that state. States that are agriculture-based are very careful about the possibility of bringing in potential "pests."

Breeding: The males have prominent scrotal sacs under their tails, literally as big as their head. (This may be an adaptation to living in a warmer climate and maintaining a viable

sperm production by having a cooler production center for the sperm.) Four to five young are in each litter, born after a gestation of 20–21 days. The young are weaned at 21–25 days, and become sexually mature at 8–12 weeks.

Females tend to be aggressive toward the males, especially when the females are pregnant. When kept in a small cage that doesn't afford hiding/escape routes, the male can be killed by the female.

Behavior: For humans, these are gentle hamsters that don't move as quickly as the other species. If your Chinese hamster gets loose and you can see it, it's easy to shoo it into an empty cardboard 12–pack, laid on its side, and then gently scoop it up in your hand from the carton. Ours spent much time in the exercise wheel, running for hours each day. When it began to store food in the short entranceway to the exercise wheel, we thought our pet was getting just a bit too obsessive-compulsive and we moved it to a wheel-less cage. But then we relented.

Other Hamster Species

European Hamster

Although lab hamsters get watched the most, hamsters in the wild haven't escaped behavior studies. For instance, the endangered European hamster, *Cricetus cricetus*, is one of the hamsters that travels far

Male Chinese hamsters are easy to sex.

and wide in its nightly forays for food and whatever else a hamster seeks when the night is dark. A study done by Urich Weinhold, of the University of Heidelberg, found that both males and females have territories. Males are highly territorial, have much bigger territory than the females, and do not occupy a single burrow. Females have smaller home ranges or search areas, which provide the minimum food and shelter needed during the reproductive period. The male does not invest in partnerships. He is considered successful because he mates with as many different females as possible. The less time he stays put in one burrow, the better off he is, reproductively speaking.

Females raise two litters a year. A female spends less time above ground than a male, and consequently spends more time with her young. In the schematic drawing of the male and female ranges, one male's range very conveniently overlapped the home range of three females. Roughly one quarter of his range was open, with no impinging female ranges—at the time.

Description: Head and body length are about 8–11 inches (20–28 cm) and adult weight is 16–21 ounces (712–908 g). The tail is short, and the feet are broad with digging claws. Fur is red-brown on the back, white on the sides, and black on the belly. You might consider the pelt very attractive, and you wouldn't be alone. It has cheek pouches, which it uses for food transport and transport of the young, and can inflate with air

A Syrian black tortoiseshell hamster.

for greater buoyancy before it crosses a stream or other body of water.

Burrows: The European hamster prefers dry sandy soil for its burrows. It will inhabit grassy steppes, plowed land, cultivated fields, and along riverbanks, from lowlands to a 2,000 feet (610 m) elevation. It has shallow burrows for summer dwelling and deeper burrows for winter. Each burrow has areas for food, sleeping, and excreta. Many hamsters' burrows may be crowded into a small area, where suitable burrowing is limited.

Food: This hamster is nocturnal, venturing out at night to collect cereal seeds, peas, potatoes, and roots. It also eats green parts of plants, insect larvae, and frogs. It is a prodigious collector of food, and may store up to 180 pounds (90 kg) of food in its burrow. You can understand why many farmers can't see the finer side of this hamster, and

The banded Syrian hamster shows how attractive a multicolored coat can be.

why its black, white, and brown pelt is an exported item (see page 24).

Hibernation: Like other hamsters, the European hamster semihibernates during cold weather. It shoves dirt into the entrance of its burrow, closing the burrow off, and retreats to a grass-lined nest. There it sleeps, waking at five- to seven-day intervals to feed off the food it has stored. Mind you, it gets cold at latitude 60°, which is about the northernmost extension of its range. During this time, its body temperature drops from 90 to 39°F (32 to 4°C).

Breeding: Breeding occurs from spring to August, with perhaps two litters being born each year. In captivity, away from the short-day/long-day cycle, breeding can occur every month. Young are born after a 16-20-day gestation, and litters are usually 4–18 (but usually 6–12). Females are sexually mature and receptive when 43 days old and can bear young when 59 days old. Their life span is about two years.

Politics and the European Hamster

The European hamster was once found across much of Europe, from Belgium across to Russia. It is also called the common hamster and the black-bellied hamster. It is now endangered throughout western Europe, Germany, the Netherlands, Belgium, and France, although not in the western part of its range.

In Europe almost half of the vertebrate species are threatened, due to habitat loss caused by intensive agricultural practices and urbanization. In 1979 a conservation-minded meeting was held in Berne, Switzerland, to protect Europe's wild flora and fauna and their habitats. From the meeting came an agreement, a set of rules and procedures called the Berne Convention. Each country that signed the agreement is considered a party to the agreement, and each country must submit a report every six years on how that country is doing in following the Convention guidelines for species protection. The European hamster is one of the endangered species covered by the Berne Convention. Its decline has made it the focus of a lot of attention.

Tracking the European hamster began in 1970 in France, just a year after the Berne Convention afforded this animal protection from collection, killing, and harassment. Up until 1994, the European hamster was found in less than 1 percent of the areas checked. Then the populations took a nosedive. By 1997 the European hamsters were found in only 10 percent of the 1994 sites.

Protecting an animal on paper is one thing; actually enforcing that protection is a whole new topic. American real estate owners generally don't like the Endangered Species Act, and German owners are no different when faced with the Berne Convention. It's due, in part, to the very human reaction to being told what one can or cannot do with one's land. The welfare of any animal, in this case the European hamster, does not always come first. The German government has allowed intensive agricultural and industrial construction in an area near the Dutch border. This area is one of three important breeding sites for the European hamster.

In 2001 the European Commission asked—for the second time—for an

A black Syrian hamster is called a teddy-bear hamster by some breeders.

explanation from Germany as to why this intensive construction had been allowed. (Germany had already distinguished itself in the eyes of the Commission by not submitting a list of protected lands, even three years after a complaint on that subject was filed.) The German representative

The winter white's ears are almost concealed in its fur.

Many color morphs of the Campbell's hamster have ruby eyes.

responded by saying there were no hamsters in that area.

The Berne Convention

The Berne Convention was held in Berne, Switzerland, in 1979. The sponsor was the Council of Europe, which wanted to create uniform conservation measures across the European continent. There are 43 members of the Convention; 32 of which are European countries.

The Convention set standards for countries to follow in regional habitat conservation and species protection. Those parties to the Convention, as they are called, agreed that there should be no catching and no killing of native species with particular respect to migratory floral or fauna. The parties also agreed there should be no deliberate destruction to resting or breeding sites, no deliberate disturbance of the animals, especially during breeding, rearing, and hibernation seasons, and no possession or internal trade of live or dead animals. Although the Convention is broad in scope, it recognizes that regional enforcement to the guidelines is critical to the plan's success.

To ensure that the guidelines are being followed, parties must submit annual reports on their implementation of the Convention provisions—but the Convention isn't a no-exceptions group. Exceptions may be invoked, basically when there is no other satisfactory solution, and when the exception will not be detrimental to the population in question.

Any party, nongovernmental organization, individual, or organization can complain to the Supervisory Committee that one of the parties is not complying. If the secretary agrees there are grounds for the complaint, a letter is sent to the party. The party must respond within four months. The secretary may decide the complaint is serious enough to take to the Supervisory Committee (the SC). The SC may open a case file, which is what has happened in the case of the European hamster habitat destruction at the Germany-Netherlands border. The SC may also decide to make an on-site appraisal (this sort of quick action is needed when an event of short duration is being threatened, such as the breeding breaches for the green turtles in Greece (another open case).

Chapter Three

Hamster Communication

Hamsters can communicate quite well with other hamsters using body posture, scent, and sounds. We puny humans are pretty much limited to interpreting just the posture and some of the sounds, but these two forms can tell you a surprising amount of what's going on in the hamster brain.

Body Language

Postural signals are an effective way to get a message across. You may remember returning home late one night and finding your parent waiting, hands on hips. Not a word is spoken but you know you're in trouble, and subsequent body communication only reinforces this initial interpretation.

Hamster body language, like the other forms of hamster-to-hamster communication, seems to deal with aggression or sexual messages. Robert E. Johnson is one of the researchers who has shared his observations of hamster postural, auditory, and chemical communication. It's a pretty sophisticated system, even if the messages are

limited. Here are the actions and what they mean:

The approach: Hamsters approach each other and lean toward each other, sniffing. They sniff-inspect each other's muzzle, from the edge of the nose to the base of the ear, where a scent gland is located on the bottom edge of the ear. The gesture reminds me of two human females, forced into a social situation and kissing the air beside each other's face and trying not to wrinkle their noses.

What hamsters learn in the approach evidently tells them the sex and perhaps the individual identity of the hamsters, since the actions that follow are appropriate to that information. Hamsters that are related sniff-ID each other for a shorter time than unrelated hamsters. A male that has been bested by another male in a fight will sniff-ID that male, and display tension in his body posture, with his ears very upright and his body leaning back from the other male. The subordinate male will then turn and depart. A female in estrus will sniff-ID, and turn to display what is tactfully described as a solicitation walk, arch her back, and assume the

Ears forward, upright posture, nose on full alert, this long-haired Syrian is waiting for someone else to make the first move.

lordosis position, which tells the male that she's interested in immediate mating.

The circle 'n sniff: The two hamsters act like two strange dogs checking each other out, circling each other, but they alternate positions in a "T" arrangement. The hamster that's the upright of the "T" sniffs the mid-regions of the other hamster (dwarf hamsters have another scent gland on the belly, just above the navel). The hamster currently sniffing may actually jam its head under the body of the other hamster, almost as if in an effort to topple the other hamster from its feet or to bite the underside. The hamsters shift positions and continue to circle while they decide which hamster will be dominant. The dominant position is the upright of the "T," the hamster with his head under the body of the first hamster. The subordinate hamster may sit back on his haunches in a more or less upright position to avoid being thrown off balance, which leads to another classic position, the face-to-face sparring.

Face-to-face sparring: The aggressor here tries to bite the subordinate's belly while the subordinate remains upright and tries to push away the aggressor. Positions tend to shift rapidly. Although it can be difficult to see who is the aggressor and who is the subordinate during these encounters, the subordinate is the one sitting more upright, with the arms and paws extended and the digits sprayed, and the mouth open. No audible signals are evident, other than some squeaking; as far as I know no work has been done to interpret these squeaks. Subordinates move in a jerky, motion-picture frame-by-frame motion, while the dominant males move quickly and smoothly. The upright posture is evidently an "alert" gesture, one used when danger threatens, because the Syrians and the European hamsters use this same posture when they sight or smell a predator.

Appeasement: Chimpanzees and gorillas use an appeasement gesture of one extended hand, eyes averted. Humans raise one hand to shoulder level, palm out, and avert their eyes, when trying to avoid a fight or disagreement. Hamsters use much the same gesture, especially when approached from the side by another hamster. The approached hamster seeks to avoid a confrontation as it holds out one paw and carefully does not look directly at the approaching hamster. It may try an appeasement called the tail flick. When appeasement doesn't work, hamsters get down to a body-to-body discussion called rolling fighting.

Rolling fighting: The aggressor may be standing upright or on all fours, as it launches an attack toward another hamster. The aggressing hamster endeavors to bite the other hamster's midsection, where the light-colored belly fur meets the darker fur of the back. The two hamsters curve their bodies around each other's midsections, and become a rolling, biting furball. This action looks serious, but it's mostly a wrestling strategy with nipping thrown in. The action halts and may end if one of the hamsters freezes in a belly-up position. The belly-up freeze may be a surrender signal.

Fighting and flying escapes: High-pitched squeaks signal an escalation of motion in a rolling furball fight. Both contestants now bite in earnest and can inflict impressive wounds on each other—and on you, if you stick your ungloved hand in to separate them.

When the discussion gets this serious, the subordinate generally tries to escape by executing a flying escape, but if the hamsters are restricted in a small cage with no hiding places, the dominant hamster

Leaning forward, head tilted back and nose forward, the Syrian is trying to figure out what to expect.

often follows and presses the attack, called the chase.

The chase: The consequences of the chase can be very serious for the subordinate hamster. Since you control the caging arrangements, you need to act, because in the wild the subordinate could escape. Startle the hamsters with a few squirts from a water sprayer, and either shoo one hamster into a tin can or reach in with your gloved hand to remove it to another cage.

Tail flick: A subordinate male may try to halt the aggression by flicking his tail upward and humping his back upward. This posture has been noted in both the Syrian and the European hamster. If the subordinate male moves, he will walk with a slower, stiff-legged gait. The dominant male

Body Language

Burrows through clean litter in the cage: It's happy and checking to see if perhaps there might be some delicious things to eat hidden away.

Watches you with ears erect: It's curious about something but pretty calm.

Grooms self: Hamster seeks reassurance that everything is fine, or hamster is content and feels that a bit of a scratch and groom would feel good.

Stretches: It's feeling good and relaxed.

Ears forward, cheek pouches puffed up: Hamster is feeling frightened.

Cheek pouches hastily emptied: Hamster may feel insecure, as if it may need to flee.

Stands on back feet and moves front arms together, almost as if it's boxing: Hamster feels threatened and is countering with aggression.

Startled when you approach cage: Hamster isn't feeling safe and could use some gentle handling over several days time and maybe a hide box in the cage.

Ears are laid back: Hamster is suspicious of something and is watching carefully; may feel aggressive or upset.

Flops onto back and displays teeth: Hamster is frightened and wants you to back off or you may get bitten.

Creeps along floor of cage, especially near the walls: Hamster feels uncertain and frightened, knows there's something bad out there.

Front foot extended, palm down—an appeasement gesture.

Buzz off! Flattened ears and indignant squeaks warn the intruder.

may respond by mounting the subordinate male. Interesting enough, when the fight is between a male and a female, and the male loses and displays the tail-up position, the female has not been observed mounting the male. The tail-up pose is often used by young hamsters that are placed in an unfamiliar nest to forestall attacks. Normally, scent cues will forestall a young hamster from entering a nest that is not its own.

Hamster-to-Human Communication

Hamsters can communicate with us in many ways. It's simply a matter of understanding their body positions. Here are a few clues—but you should be able to add a few of your own, after you've spent a few months watching and playing with your hamster.

Auditory Communication

You've heard your hamsters squeak as they wander about their cage, and you've certainly heard Syrians squeak if placed together. Your hamster may squeak when you pick it up. If you restrain it by the scruff of the neck, it may squeak and briefly struggle.

If you pay attention when your hamster vocalizes, you'll understand part of what's going on in its world, but only part. Much hamster vocalization is ultrasonic. Infant hamsters, in particular, utilize sounds that may

Are you sure that you're not a threat? A wary hamster narrows its eyes and puts its ears back.

be entirely ultrasonic or partially sonic, to elicit maternal care from the adults.

Adults produce short calls, just 60 to 170 milliseconds (a millisecond is one-thousandth of a second). The longer duration is just shy of ⅙th of a second, so even those vocalizations that are sonic are of such a short duration your hearing may not pick

Now you've done it, and I'm really angry! A ready-to-fight hamster puffs its cheeks, opens its mouth and put its ears foward.

Ears tucked flat, body flattened, this normal Campbell's is creeping around until it figures out what's going on.

A quick grooming is comforting.

up on them. Some of the calls don't vary in frequency, while the others vary in modulation. O. R. Floody and D. W. Pfaff worked with hamster vocalizations during the 1970s and found that the vocalizations appear to be sexually oriented, functioning to attract a mate and to instigate mating behavior. (The same is true in frogs.)

Mating Calls

The females call most frequently when they are in estrus. Females rarely call when lactating, or when the days are short (the equivalent of winter, when food in the wild would be hard to find). In females, high calling rates are dependent on high levels of estrogen followed by progesterone, the same hormonal sequence that determines lordosis (the mating invitation position) and receptivity. The

calls of the females could be heard in the open air at a distance of 36 to 76 feet (11 to 23 m), but no work was done at the time of this investigation to determine if the sound would carry underground, in a tunnel system. If a female were actively seeking a mate, it seems most logical that she'd be out in the open, broadcasting her interest. Calling by males is also influenced by hormonal levels.

Both males and females are stimulated to call ultrasonically when they smell or see members of the opposite sex. Exactly what odor stimulates the females to call when they scent a male isn't known, although females call a lot less when the male in question has been castrated, indicating at least some involvement of androgen.

When the female sees the male, she stops calling and goes into

Baby Syrians huddle to conserve warmth and communicate with audible and inaudible squeaks.

lordosis. If the male wanders off, she comes out of lordosis and begins calling again. Males, once they briefly encounter a female in estrus, change their calls. This new call is still different from the calls produced by a male in contact with a female in lordosis, sort of an "Aha!" call as opposed to "Eureka!"

Obviously, finding a mate in the wild takes more work than finding a mate in a communal caging system.

The Teeth Chatter

Fear and aggression are evidenced by the teeth chatter, made by repeatedly clicking the teeth together. Male-male encounters produce the highest percentage of teeth chatters, although female-female encounters

also result in chattering. When one hamster intrudes into another hamster's cage, the intruder's teeth chatter, either out of nervousness or as an appeasement gesture, but Robert Johnston notes that it can be very difficult to tell which hamster is doing the chattering.

Echo Location

Can hamsters use ultrasound as an echo-location device, especially in dark burrows? It's an interesting thought. Shrews use ultrasound in exploration and navigation, and shrews have poor eyesight, just like hamsters. To date, no use of ultrasound has been found when a hamster is placed in an unfamiliar situation, although the possibility of

All hamsters rely more on scent than on sight to tell them what's out there.

their using ultrasound as a choice does exist.

Chemical Cues

Hamsters communicate very specific messages via their scent glands, which vary in location and number from species to species.

Flank Scent Glands

The mesocritcetan hamsters (the Syrian, the Romanian, and the Turkish hamsters) and the Roborovski hamsters have paired flank scent glands, one high on each hip. The hip glands are visible on the unfurred young, but are soon hidden by the growing fur.

The flank glands are sexually dimorphic, with those of the males being about twice the size of the females' 2–4 mm-long flank glands. The glands are androgen-dependent, meaning they become smaller if the male is castrated and larger if the castrated male is given supplementary androgen. The flank glands of the males secrete pheromones, scented hormones that are used in signaling members of the opposite sex, and become visibly damp when the males become sexually excited. Microscopically, the glands contain enlarged specialized sebaceous glands.

The glands are used to mark territory. Hamsters rub the sides of the body against vertical surfaces in their caging, much as a dog will rub his body along a wall after it has rolled in mud. Scent from the flank glands is probably also deposited on the floor of the cage, since hamsters scratch their flanks with their hind paws.

Flank marking occurs both in nonsocial and social contexts. Nonsocial contexts may be as the hamsters enter or leave their nest area, or before or after grooming, and seem almost a casual afterthought. Social contexts are more intense, when they smell other hamsters of the same species or are put into contact with them. Like bears, male hamsters are stirred to mark their territory when they discover the marking of another male hamster.

Flank marking is also a status and agonistic, or antagonistic, indicator. Dominant hamsters mark more frequently than subordinate hamsters, even in same-sex pairings or same-sex quads. In a study of paired males, the subordinate male marked very rarely, and then it was in or adjacent to his nest, as if to protect/mark it against intrusion.

When exposed to estrous females (females ready to breed), male flank marking decreases. Females in their estrous cycle reduce their own marking process when they encounter odors from males. This reduction in marking of both sexes when mating appears imminent reinforces the concept that the marking is an aggressive gesture.

Other Scent Glands

The dwarf hamsters, the Campbell's hamster, and the winter white hamster have six pairs of scent glands, located on the ears, the belly, and the genitals.

• Campbell's have a specialized scent gland on the belly, just anterior to the naval. Males can be seen to touch the floor of their cages with their bellies, as if marking, and female hamsters mark their area by pressing their genitals against the floor of the cage with the tail upraised.

• The male winter white's ventral scent gland has been found to contain 48 different compounds. The same gland in the female doesn't contain enough secretions for analysis; this indicates that the gland has a definite sexual identification function.

• Hamsters' ear glands are on the bottom side of the external ear. Females' ear glands are smaller than those of the males, although the glands will grow if they are injected with testosterone. Males spend more time sniffing at the females' ear gland scent than at the scent from male ear glands.

The paired scent glands are visible on young Syrians.

Campbell's slink around, both to reduce their own visibility and to leave their scent via their ventral scent glands.

Following a trail—a Campbell's hamster finds there's already been another hamster in this very spot.

• The harderian glands, which are found behind the eye in hamsters and many other animals including deer, have been credited with assisting in a wide variety of functions, including eye lubrication, photoreception (detection of light), maintenance of coat, and body temperature regulation. The glands may also be a source of pheromones, assist with function of the pineal gland (which in turn helps with night and day cycles), and in melatonin manufacture (melatonin appears to play a role in sleep). The harderian glands are larger in male hamsters than in females. In gerbils, secretions from the harderian glands travel through tear ducts and are spread about the face during grooming. It would seem likely that the same occurs in hamsters, and it is partially the harderian gland scent that hamsters are sniffing when they identify another hamster in facial sniffing.

Salivary Glands

The chemistry in the salivary gland secretions from the winter white hamster differs from male to female. You can say, with fair accuracy, that a hamster's very breath plays a role in individual recognition.

Chapter Four

Caging

Hamster caging can be expensive or inexpensive, lavish or plain. As long as a few basic parameters are met, your hamster will live its allotted two to three years as a contented and busy hamster who's lucky enough to have a doting owner.

Your hamster needs a safe cage that provides room to run around in and things to do, food, a place to sleep, a place to defecate, and clean water.

None of these are particularly hard to supply. The only caveat you need to remember is that hamsters are chewers and escape artists (Israel Aharoni, page 7, learned the hard way. You don't have to). Hamsters can, if they decide they want to, chew through wood or soft plastic, such as the plastic screening on a tank top. Try to provide a cage that at least is difficult to chew out of, and provide "play" items such as branches and pieces of wood to chew on.

Materials and Styles

There are many ready-made cage designs that are well suited for your hamster. Wire mesh or wire-barred cages are both good choices. Just make certain the bars are closely enough spaced so your hamster can't wriggle through, and this means bars spaced at a half-inch (13 mm) or less. If you're planning on breeding your hamster, or if you get a female hamster that has been housed communally in a pet store, you'll need to opt for a more solid

Wire cages can be purchased that fit atop aquariums (courtesy Quality Cage Company: www.qualitycage.com).

cage, one that has the bars too high up for the babies to reach until they are too big to get between them. To put it gently, once a dwarf or even a baby Syrian is out of its cage, it's decidedly difficult to track down and recapture (see page 63 if you're already at this point).

There's one style of mesh caging that fits on top of an aquarium. A ramp runs from a shelf in the mesh cage to the bottom of the aquarium. The exercise wheel is included in the mesh portion. This cage gives a hamster both a draft-free bottom portion and a lot of climbing space.

Doors: Be certain that any door can be securely latched. Hamsters, or any other small rodent, are perfectly capable of doing what you might consider an amazing feat of lifting a sliding door open with their front feet, and

You may be able to adapt caging that is already on hand for your hamster.

then scampering happily behind your largest and most heavily laden bookcase.

Size: Walk right past the cute little cages that are smaller in size than a 5-gallon (19-L) terrarium. If manufacturers think there's market for a small cage, they'll make it, but just because the cage has been manufactured, and is for sale, doesn't make it a good cage for your hamster. Although lab hamsters are required to have a 10 × 10-inch (25 × 25 cm) area per hamster, remember that hamsters evolved as vagabonds. Provide a roomy cage for your hamster, the biggest one you can afford, both money and space-wise.

Hamsters like to move around, especially at night. Don't obligate yourself by saying "I'll let it out every night for exercise"; that's not fair to either of you. A cage that is 12 inches wide by 15 inches long by 12 inches high (30 × 38 × 30 cm) would be fine for one or two dwarf hamsters, or for a single Syrian. You can increase the cage's living area and make it more interesting if you add an exercise wheel, ramps, and second-level tunnels; these can be added using premade cage accessories or you can make your own (see page 62).

Hamsters with sufficiently large cages substantially reduce the amount of time spent in the wheel. Even after you have your caging set up, if your hamster spends considerable time in the wheel, you might rethink the size of the cage you've provided. Although some hamster

There are also lots of commercial caging types to choose from.

keepers (and some researchers) feel the endless wheel is obsessive, they themselves aren't confined to a small room for their lifetime.

Recycled Converted Caging

You may not need to buy caging for your hamster. Hamsters can live well and prosper in recycled or converted caging, caging you may already have on hand from other pets. But I'd admit the commercial hamster cages look appealing, and they seem to offer a lot for a hamster to do.

Bird cages: Bird cages make adaptable hamster caging, providing that the bars are close enough together to avoid any escapes, and that you secure all the sliding doors, even those over the feeding cups. Give your hamster credit for persistence. You may think you've wedged

all those doors shut so only you can open them, but you aren't in a cage 24 hours a day with nothing to do but worry about a possible escape route. (If you haven't heard the stories that begin, "My kid had a hamster and one day it got out...," you will.) Buy sliding latches, the kind that are on dog leashes, and use them on each door. Hamsters aren't strong enough to push the slide back. Those plastic feeding dishes that come with a bird cage would work well for your hamster's food, as long as you know that your hamster will probably move most of the food into the bed where it can keep a very close eye on it—there's nothing personal here; it's just a hamster thing.

Bird cages are tall enough to add an exercise wheel and ramps. If the cage has a wire grid above the bottom—some hamster cages are *sold*

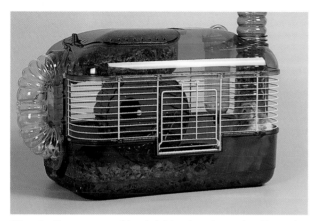

The plastic cages combine bright colors, barred walls, and crawling tubes.

with these grids—remove the grid so your hamster can wander about on the floor of the cage without hurting its feet. The bars are too far apart to permit your hamster to wander about on the cage floor with any sort of comfort (it's like asking to you to walk barefoot across a floor littered

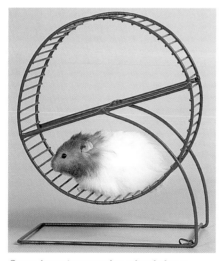

Some hamster exercise wheels have crossbars.

with pencils), and all the seeds, treats, and stolen food items will fall though the bars where your pet can't reach them. Researchers have found that hamsters show a strong preference for solid-floor cages with bedding over barren, wire mesh-floored cages, in case you wondered.

Multicolored Cages

The plastic hamster cages go by a variety of names, most of which incorporate the word "trail." These multicolored cages come in bright colors and offer a wire or plastic top that clicks onto a plastic base. Add-on (at additional cost) plastic tubes snake out of one side and connect to another side or to the top, to special viewing bins on the side or a top-side access panel. If you have a Syrian hamster, especially if the hamster is even the least bit chubby, make certain that these tubes are sufficiently large. All those I've seen include an exercise wheel, but plan to add one if your caging doesn't come with it. Again, buy the biggest cage you can.

These cages seem to be the impetus for a veritable explosion of accessories beyond the tubes. Manufacturers have spared nothing in bringing out colored water bottles that hang on the outside of the cage, plastic viewing hemisphere bubbles, extra snap-on running wheels, and plastic sleeping houses. They've even created rolling hamster balls and hamster motorcycles (this one is powered by an exercise wheel). The cages afford several areas for

Temporary Housing

Plastic shoeboxes or sweater boxes can be used for temporary or travel hamster cages, if you add circulation. The easiest way to do this is by cutting pieces out of the side and the top, and riveting in eighth-inch pieces of hardware cloth to cover the holes. You can drill additional holes in the sides. A water bottle will go on the top, with the drinking tube being pushed through the wire mesh so the hamster can reach the tube to drink.

These cages are fine for a day or two, but they aren't good for permanent housing, they are too low for the hammie to stand on its hind legs. Also, neither the shoebox nor the sweater box is high enough for an exercise wheel, and there's no room for toys in the shoebox. Low boxes are suitable only for temporary housing.

hamsters to explore and perch. If you keep communal types such as Campbell's or winter whites, you can use the tunnels to connect their cages. When I found I was mentally planning how to run tunnels around the top of one of my rooms, rather like the toy trains that chug around in some restaurants, I shook myself and said, "Enough. Really. At least for now."

If you do buy one of the rolling hamster balls, or the rolling hamster-powered motorcycle, don't let your hamster use them unsupervised on a warm day, or on a sunny day, in a room with lots of windows. These exercise "wheels" have no water source, and your hamster could become too warm if allowed to stay in the wheel too long.

The colorful cages are available in several sizes, are easy to clean, and provide a decorative alternative to older types of hamster housing. They have a multitude of doors that provide easy access but they stymied my own hamster. As with the all-wire cages, the hamster can push shredded bedding through the barred areas, but that tends to be a minor problem. The barred sections provide splendid ventilation.

Aquariums

You might consider using an aquarium. Many pet stores use them as display tanks, and aquariums were the caging of choice for many years. An aquarium with a wire mesh topper cage may offer the best of both worlds.

Aquariums by themselves have solid walls that contain odors along with the animals within (older hamster how-to guides, copying from even earlier, pre-antibiotic days, solemnly caution against a hamster getting chilled). Aquariums are fairly easy to clean, although they are heavy. An aquarium is high enough to add an exercise wheel. It has corners, which hamsters like. It's almost escape-proof; hamsters can't climb glass, but if they can clamber atop sleeping boxes or up a watering bottle to scramble out over the top of a cage, they'll sure do it.

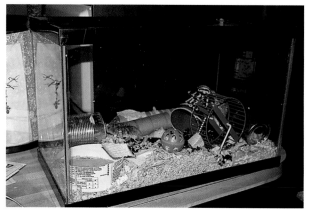
Aquariums provide draft-free housing.

To me, the plain aquarium's claim to fame as a hamster house is also its detriment. Yes, those solid sides mean your hamster won't get chilled, but honestly, exactly how cold is your house during the winter? I'm willing to bet your home's interior doesn't dip below 60°F (15.6°C), even at night. How is a hamster, nestled inside his hamster house with a bed of freshly shredded unscented tissues, going to get chilled? Aquariums don't permit any air circulation. How is your hamster going to know what's going on (hamsters live in an olfactory world, see page 40)? Inside a glass house, how is your hamster going to be able to stick his little nose out to gather a snootful of the latest news, or be able to hear you say, "Listen up here, real peanut comin' in on your left," and then hear you make airplane noises as you deliver the promised treat? Inside a glass house, a hamster has to live with his own odor, particularly if you don't

clean his litter pan every other day or so.

If you use an aquarium for a hamster cage, you don't really need to cover it, unless there are objects the hamster can use as a stairway to freedom, or unless there are other animals in your apartment or house. I've seen both dogs and cats perform astonishing acts of agility to get close enough to stick their big fat noses into a hamster cage. A wire screen top will forestall such familiarity. Another advantage of covering the tank is that you can't accidentally drop other things into it.

Setting Up the Cage

Water

Hamsters must have clean water available to them at all times. In a pinch, you can offer water in a small crock or plastic jaw lid, but this isn't going to work long-term. Hamsters fill up water dishes with whatever they can find in their cage, rather on the cheerful attitude of, "Well! Let's just bustle right in and fix that big wet spot and keep this cage from getting soggy!"

Go out and buy a laboratory water bottle. They are plastic or, rarely, glass bottles, with a hard rubber cork or a screw top and a metal drinking tube. You fill the bottle with water, screw on the top or wedge the cork in the mouth, and hook the bottle on the side of the cage or perch it on the top.

The drinking tube extends into the cage at a level where the hamster can reach it and your hamster has fresh water for a week or so. At the end of a week, or when the bottle is about half empty, you take it down, clean it, refill it, and put it back in place.

If you notice that your hamster chews on the water bottle, it means one of three things:

1. The bottle is empty.

2. Somehow the bottle has become plugged and your hamster can't get any water.

3. Your hamster needs something to chew on because it likes to chew and it's bored.

Check the water bottle, and fill it if it's empty. If the substrate is wet, change it! Put in a few lengths of branches (apple, pear, or orange are particularly good, if you can find a source), some rat chow, some hamster seed mix, and an alfalfa cube/timothy hay or hamster toys to chew on.

Food Dishes

You can buy nice ceramic or metal food dishes for your hamster, but your hamster won't use them very much. It may not feel the need to move the timothy hay, but it will probably relocate the seed mixture. Most hamsters prefer the area right next to the bed for food. This means, of course, when you clean the cage you throw a lot of food away. If you have a compost pile, you can dump the shavings there and if it rains you have a nice green sprouted compost bed.

A lab watering bottle keeps the water fresh and accessible (courtesy Quality Cage Company: www.qualitycage.com).

When I kept my hamsters in a tiered cage rack, I found a combined food dispenser/toy that reminded me of the pigeon experiments, where a pigeon is trained to peck at a lever and is rewarded by food when the correct lever is chosen. The food dispenser had three compartments, each controlled by a lever. I filled the compartments with hamster diet, sunflower seeds, and wild bird seed, and put the container into a cage with a family of dwarf hamsters. They went nuts over it, pressing the levers clunk, clunk, clunk, and moving out the food until the device was empty. They seemed

Plastic exercise wheels can be added to plastic cages.

Two Types of Litter Not to Use and Why

Clumping kitty litters: Hamsters are coprophagic, which means that, like rabbits, they eat a portion of their feces as part of the digestive process. (This is explained in the diet section, and it's no weirder than a cow chewing its cud.) If ingested along with the feces or even the food, the clay lodges in the hamster's digestive system and your hamster will die of intestinal obstruction. In addition, clay kitty litter is so drying it will cause your hamster's feet to become chapped and cracked.

Cedar-based shavings and litters: Many hamster keepers don't use cedar in any form. They feel that the aromatic oils—the phenols—are irritating to the hamster's respiratory system. They point out that when cedar is used in the cage, the hamster has no escape; the hamster has to breathe the fumes 24 hours a day. There are anecdotal accounts of neurological damage and convulsions. Yes, pet stores still sell cedar shavings. The shavings do smell good, unless you have to smell them all day and all night. Just because something is for sale for use by hamsters, or rather, their owners, it doesn't mean that item is the best thing to use. You may have to evaluate some products yourself.

less interested in actually eating the food than playing with the device, another reason I soon moved them to a larger, barred cage. The food compartments were so small that they had to be filled twice daily, one reason I gave up on it once my hamsters were in better caging.

Substrate, or Flooring for All

Hamsters are burrowing creatures, and your hamster will be much happier if it has something to burrow in. There's not much difference between a substrate—something that goes on the floor of the cage—and bedding, in most cages. If you use a substrate that will hold a tunnel's shape, as do pine or aspen shavings, your hamster can burrow through the substrate to his heart's content, and pile it up wherever it likes for its sleeping area.

Newspapers: If it's ten o'clock at night and you've just walked in the door with your new hamster, you don't have to go out and search for substrate. Torn strips of newspaper over a solid sheet of newspaper will work. A bit of warning, however—a hamster kept in a cage with newspaper substrate will spend its time ripping and shredding the newspaper to fluff it up, and it will get covered with rubbed-off news ink. Try to avoid this sort of extra mess.

Paper towels: Another "at-home" choice is paper towels, placed on the bottom of the cage and torn into strips, which your hamster will fussily shred to its liking. Paper towels tend to compact quickly, but they are absorbent and easy to replace.

Shredded paper: One of my friends pointed proudly to her cage that was half filled with shredded paper. "I bought a paper shredder" she said. "I don't have to buy any substrate anymore. I can make all I need." You can buy shredded paper krinkles as well, but whether you buy them or use shredded documents, the shredded papers don't absorb worth a hoot. Not only are you and your hamster looking at, and walking in (well, your hamster, anyway), a cage with liquid garbage on the floor, but the cage is going to smell as well. Even every-other-day cage changes aren't going to kill the odor, and one of the main purposes behind substrate is to absorb odor.

Commercial choices: Your pet store is a good place to check out what's available in substrate. You'll

Paper krinkles look great, from a human perspective, but they are nonabsorbent.

see pine shavings, pine pellets, aspen shavings, aspen pellets, alfalfa pellets (also known as rabbit food), pecan pellets, sawdust, corncob bits, ground walnut or pecan shells, shredded wheat stems, shredded hibiscus stems, recycled newspaper, coconut husk fiber, and cypress mulch, all of which will work to a greater or lesser degree. I urge you to try them all, and to retry them at intervals. Your hamster needs cage enrichment, remember, and cleaning a cage is a bit less boring for you if you have something new to try. Many of these products are sold in the pet departments of your local grocery store; while others are sold primarily or exclusively in pet stores. When you find one or two you really like, look into on-line ordering in bulk, so you can keep perhaps a two-month supply on hand. Be sure to check freight charges, so you'll know how much you're actually spending.

Pine or aspen shavings: For most owners, the easiest substrate is pine or aspen shavings. You can buy bags of both kinds at your pet or discount store, or you can buy pine shavings by the 3-cubic feet bale at your local feed store (it's used in horse stalls). I've heard warnings that the stuff sold for horse stalls "might" be contaminated with rodent feces, but I don't believe a word of it. The shavings can be placed in a thick enough layer to allow your pet to stay hidden while it sleeps and it can cunningly sneak from side to side in the cage and poke its head up to observe you when you aren't paying attention to it—and you thought you got a hamster so you could have fun watching *it*!

Pelleted substrates: The pelleted substrates are very good at controlling odors and absorption, but the only binder used for the pellets is water, so once they get wet, they fall apart into sawdust. They do help keep the cage fresh, but they don't hold the shape of a burrow when a hamster has tunneled through them. I used pecan pellets, and didn't think they absorbed as much moisture as the pine or aspen pellets, but that's only my opinion. Pellets are also heavier than wood shavings or shredded paper, and it's harder to toss them out of the cage or push them through the bars (I said harder, not impossible). Some have additives such as baking soda, enzymes, or other products. Read the labels before you buy a product, and avoid those that have odors added. If you have any doubts, call the manufacturer and ask someone in the public relations department about the safety of their product when used with hamsters; if they can't tell you, that's enough of an answer. If a product isn't safe for your pet, you don't want to waste your money.

Corncob bits: Corncob bits are an attractive pale beige color, but I did not find them to be very moisture- or odor-absorbent. Hamsters can only shove them around; they aren't any good for burrowing.

Shredded wheat grass: The shredded wheat grass is one of the newer substrates. It's lightweight, has high absorbency due to its high surface-to-mass ratio, and is a pale tan color. Like other pourable substrates, it won't hold a burrow's shape, so you'll want to add some cardboard tubes. If you have more than a cage or two of hamsters, you'll find that this substrate is more expensive than some of the others. The makers point out that it's digestible if it gets ingested, and it certainly has no odor of its own. My hamster seemed to enjoy shoving it around, and I liked its odor and moisture-controlling properties.

The shredded hibiscus substrate is labeled for use in lizard cages, but it works well in hamster cages. It absorbs more moisture than pine shavings, but one 8-ounce (224 g) bag provided enough for only two of my hamster cages. For about the same amount of money, I could get 3 cubic feet of pine shavings, enough for all eight of my hamster cages, twice over. This is too bad, because I really liked the shredded hibiscus stem, partly because it seemed to be very odor-absorbent (I had eight cages of hamsters in my front room at the time), and it was easier to pour it into the hamster cages than shoving in handfuls of shavings. It doesn't provide any burrowing opportunities, so you might want to add some form of substitute burrows, such as cardboard tubing.

Recycled newspapers: Another of the newer substrates is recycled newspapers. One brand looks like twisted bits of gray paper, and it's very odor- and moisture-absorbent. It's treated so any non-soy inks left in the pulp can't harm your hamster and it absorbs liquids quite well. It doesn't hold the shape of a burrow at all, but the hamsters seem to enjoy shoving it around.

Taking the Cage Home

When you get your caging and accessories home, or you take the cage out of your storage area, wash the cage down with a mild soap and water, and rinse and dry it. Now you're ready to set up the caging.

Provide a sleeping area: Hamsters in the wild hollow out just a small room in their burrow to use as a sleeping area. They like to feel cozy while they sleep, so when they are in a cage, they'll try to find a corner to use, and they add something

soft and shredded to "snug up" the room. Offer your hamster a small sleeping room, one large enough for the hamster to turn around in. I've used a small tin can, with one end cut out and the edges smoothed, and a small cardboard box with a hamster-sized entry hole cut into it, or I've cut down empty tissue boxes and used them.

Any of a variety of small containers will work; a small terra-cotta flowerpot, turned upside down with an opening nipped out, small bits at a time, at the bottom edge with a pair of pliers works fine. A tiny finch nesting basket can be fastened to the side of the cage so it won't roll. You want whatever sort of house you provide to be big enough for your hamster, to have some ventilation, and to be easy to clean or throw away if it becomes soiled.

But be cautious: Don't use a box too small to turn around in. I gave a pair of my prettiest Campbell's an empty film box. Two days later, I

A terra-cotta flower pot makes a good sleeping area.

Finch or other small baskets can be used for hamster beds.

found one of my hamsters quite dead in it, his face jammed into a corner. He probably suffocated. Captive-bred hamsters aren't smart, and if they can't turn around, they'll keep trying to go forward. Backing up may not be something they can think of when they're in a tight spot.

Empty toilet paper rolls or sections of empty paper towel rolls make good sleeping areas, and they are easy to get out of; the hamster just walks through them.

Your hamsters may or may not accept a sleeping box. I provided sleeping boxes of several designs, only to have them studiously ignored. They didn't want the wooden boxes, the cardboard boxes, or even the store-bought sleeping house, filled with brightly colored paper krinkles. The hamsters preferred to sleep in their shredded tissue heaps. This may have less to do with the quality or design of the

sleeping boxes offered than the ambient temperature. I live in Florida, where a summertime room temperature of 80°F (26.7°C) is an affordable goal. The close quarters of a sleeping box may have been too warm for fur-covered hamsters.

Whether or not your hamster accepts a sleeping box or remains a purist and wants only tissues, it's easy to replace only the bedding once or twice a week and change the cage substrate every one or two weeks.

Adding the food dish: Add at least one food dish, one for timothy hay and perhaps another for the seed mix/kibble that forms the other part of their diet. You can easily get by with one feeding dish, the one for the hay, because hamsters don't like to leave food in a feeding dish and will generally shove it out of the dish and move it elsewhere.

Ramps and platforms: Hamsters enjoy exploring their cage when they awaken, and the addition of a few ramps and platforms will greatly increase the available floor space. If your cage doesn't have these built in, you can check with your local pet store for proper hamster ramps. These snap into place and are generally quite serviceable. If your local store doesn't stock ramps, you can build some using items found at your local home improvement store. I've made ramps from unfinished ¼ × 3-inch (6 mm × 7.6 cm) hobbyist wood strips, from strips of ½ × 1-inch (13 mm × 2.5 cm) hardware cloth and from perforated aluminum soffit strips. All the types I made worked well and were used by the hamsters. The metal ones had an advantage in that they couldn't get chewed up, but that's an advantage from my viewpoint only. Maybe my hamsters liked chewing up the wooden ramps; it took them the better part of a month to render the ramps unsightly, and they were quite persevering in their work. It was only a matter of 20 minutes to build some new ones.

Hint: If you're going to try the wooden ramps, build a couple of extras when you're building the first, so you can replace them easily if they get chewed up. I always discovered cage renovations were needed at night, when the stores were closed and I had two packed days in front of me. Having a few extra ramps on hand was a real help.

Exercise wheels: Hamsters love exercise wheels. I think these are important for keeping any hamster busy and exercised. If your caging doesn't have room for an exercise wheel, rethink your caging. My Chinese hamster loved his exercise wheel so much that he moved in a bit of food, I guess to snack on when he got hungry. His cage went squeak, squeak, clatter, clatter all night. Then he pulled in some shredded bedding, maybe to make catching naps a little more comfortable, so his cage went squeak, clatter, swish, until I greased the wheel with Vaseline. Then he spent the better part of 20 minutes trying to pull in an empty paper towel roll, only to fail in

Even the bird department in your pet store can provide hamster caging accessories.

the end. Now his wheel goes only clatter, swish, having lost its squeak, but he seems O.K. with that.

Water bottle: Wash out the water bottle, fill it, and suspend it from the side of the cage so the hamster can drink from a standing position. Take a moment to admire the cage; it will rarely look this neat again.

Hamsters like to burrow, so provide plenty of substrate.

Porkchop became so fond of his running wheel that he slept in it.

Putting the Hamster into the Cage

1. Open the cage door, or, if you're using a cage where the top comes off, you may find it easier to handle everything if you take the top of the cage off; at least it will be easier to put the hamster inside that way, rather than trying to cram your hamster-laden hand through the fairly small door.

2. Take your hamster out of its travel box (hold it firmly so your pet won't drop to the tabletop and run; see page 77 for advice on the three basic hamster holds), talk to it, and put it in the cage.

3. Once it's inside, close the door or replace the top and take a moment to tell your hamster that it

has a new cage, a new owner, and a new life. Give it a half-day or so to settle down, although it may take considerably less time.

4. Every time you go by the cage, even if your hamster is asleep, stop and talk to it for a moment or so. You want it to get used to the sound of your voice and to the idea of seeing you at regular intervals. Expect to see your hamster regarding you gravely through the sides of the cage the first night you have it. The next day, take it out and handle it for 15 minutes or so, and daily after that, for about half an hour. You want your hamster to learn to associate you with being petted, eating good things, being out of the cage, and generally having a good time.

Litter pan: Once your hamster has been in the cage for a day or two, you'll be able to find the area it has chosen to use as a toilet. Make it easy to clean this area without disrupting the hamsters by "installing" a removable container, sort of a litter pan. I used the bottom of an orange juice carton, trimmed off about an inch high.

1. To install the litter pan, remove the soiled litter from the cage, but keep a tablespoon or so of the soiled litter and put it into the litter pan. This will help your hammie figure out what the container is for.

2. Add some fresh litter to the litter pan and put it in the cage, in the appropriate corner. Every second day or so, empty the litter pan, replace the litter, and put it back into place.

3. Once your hamster has used his litter pan, it will greatly cut down on the frequency you'll need to clean the entire cage. (Interestingly enough, even the less social Syrians hoard food communally and urinate communally.)

4. Scoop out the bathroom area every second day or so, and add fresh substrate.

Cleaning Precautions

Pay attention to where you stash your hamster while you clean its cage. When I cleaned my hamster's cage recently, I put Maudie, my yellow-black hamster, in a tall bucket with pine shavings, the same way I always do. She usually curls up and goes back to sleep. As always, I put the bucket on my kitchen table to keep my dogs from hanging their panting faces over the edge.

I heard Maudie jumping up and down in the bucket as I cleaned her cage, and she seemed agitated when I lifted her out and put her in her cleaned cage. I mentioned Maudie's agitation to my husband, Dick. He said, "Well of course, that's the bucket I used when I caught the shrew in our yard yesterday." Mind you, Maudie is many generations removed from the wild, and she has never been exposed to a shrew—until now. It's interesting to conjecture that she was responding to the odor of an enemy she's never met!

Cleaning the Cage

Once a week or so, change the substrate in your hamster's cage. If you have no place to stash your pet, try letting it run around in your bathtub while its cage is being cleaned (close the drain, of course), or you can empty your tallest kitchen trash can and put your hamster in that.

Dump the substrate and the bedding. If the cage still smells, wash the tray and bottom part of the cage with soapy water, and rinse. Wash the food dishes and the water dish (if you use one), and change the water in the bottle. A quick dry with paper towels, and you can add new substrate, replace the newly filled food dishes and water source, new

Maudie, my yellow-black Syrian, became distressed during her cage cleaning.

bedding, and you're done. Gently scoop up your hamster, pet it for a moment, and tell it what a splendid beast it is. Put it back in the cage. You can reward it, if you like, with a bit of carrot. You may reward yourself with the rest of the carrot, or go for a more complex carbohydrate in the form of carrot cake.

Interesting enough, changing a hamster's cage is supposed to be disrupting for the animal. Several researchers have done studies on the distressing effects of cage cleaning upon hamsters, but I can't vouch for the aesthetic value of hamster caging in a lab (those cages may well be the minimum 10 inches [25 cm] square), other than to say the ones I've seen are extremely plain. I never noticed my hamsters exhibiting any signs of distress at being plopped back into a cleaned cage

(except once—and the upset was caused by where I placed my hamster while I cleaned her cage—see note on page 57). If you worry about this, you can probably reduce your worry level by changing the bedding box/the loose bedding and the litter pan more frequently than you change the entire cage.

When you clean your hamster's cage you'll have to decide for yourself whether to scoop up and put the food stash back in the newly cleaned cage. After a few cautious sniffs, I just figured my hamster had probably already urinated on it, and he was going to have to create another stash. I cold-heartedly scooped out the food, the bedding, and the substrate, and replaced it with new.

Housing Hamsters in a Small Area

Rack System

If you plan to raise hamsters, you may want to create a rack system from 2 × 4s (61 × 122 cm), 1 × 2s (30 × 61 cm), casters, and kitty litter pans. This sort of system has a footprint of only 8 square feet (243 cm), which means you can keep a good number of hamsters and use up only a 2 × 4-foot (61 × 122 cm) floor space. The concept is Spartan, with a few obvious limitations. The trays are easy to clean, but the caging is not something you'd really like to have in your living room or den.

Once the water bottles are half emptied (they lie on top of the hardware cloth that forms the lid of each tray), the hamsters can't lap water from them. Another not-so-good point is that these cages don't offer any vertical space for an exercise wheel. The low layered boxes mean that the hamsters can peer through only the top for a bit of visual stimulation (mostly of the tray above them). Hamsters kept in these cages tend to spend their days rearranging their shavings, and playing with their toys, all the more reason for you to provide a stimulating cage environment, with changing the toys in each cage weekly, and changing the position of the trays within the rack weekly (but at different times than changing the toys).

To build a rack system, you'll need the following materials:
• 4 2 × 4s, 6½-feet (1.98 m) long
• 14 36-inch (91 cm) lengths of 1 × 2s
• 21 23-inch (58 cm) lengths of 1 × 2s
• 7 pieces of 24-inch (61 cm) wide quarter-inch hardware cloth, 36 × 23 inches (91 × 58 cm)
• 21 24 inch (61 cm) lengths of ½ × 1 molding
• 7 24-inch (61 cm) lengths of ⅜-inch (9.5 mm) plywood, cut in strips 2½-inches (6.25 cm) wide
• 14 24-inch (61 cm) lengths of ⅜-inch (9.5 mm) plywood, cut in strips 2 inches (5.1 cm) wide
• 6 3-foot (91 cm) lengths of ⅜ × 2 (9.5 × 51 mm) plywood to use for braces

• 4 3-inch (7.6 cm) casters
• 14 kitty litter pans, 15½ × 22¼ × 6 inches (38 × 56 × 15 cm) deep
• Staple gun and ½-inch (1.25 cm) staples; 1 ½-inch (3.8 cm) nails
• 1¼-inch-long (6.3 mm) screws (I used a screw attachment on my drill to speed assembly)

(**Note:** All wood must be untreated, because hamsters may chew on it.)

1. Assemble the frames that will serve as tops for the hamster trays. Use three 24-inch (61 cm) and two 36-inch 1 × 2s (30 × 61 cm) for each frame, and put the shorter pieces inside the longer pieces. Secure with screws or nails.

2. Staple the hardware cloth on the bottom of each frame.

A cage rack enables you to house a lot of hamsters in a relatively small area.

3. Add the suspension runners. Place a ½ × 1-inch (1.25 × 2.5 cm) 24-inch (61 cm) length of molding atop the hardware cloth, aligned with the 23-inch (58 cm) 1 × 2s (30 × 61 cm). Nail in place.

4. Add the 24-inch (61 cm) strips of ⅜-inch (9.5 mm) plywood over the molding on each side, outside edges aligned.

5. Add the 2½-inch (6.25 cm) wide strip of ⅜-inch (9.5 mm) plywood to the molding piece in the center. Center this piece so a lip extends equally along each side.

6. Now you'll fasten the frames to the 2 × 4s (61 × 122 cm). Starting at the top of each 2 × 4, make pencil marks at 10-inch (25 cm) intervals.

7. You'll assemble the unit on its back. Place two of the 2 × 4s narrow side up, 23 inches (58 cm) apart. Place one of the frames (which will be the top frame), vertically between the 2 × 4s.

8. Put screws through the 2 × 4s, securing them to the frame. Put the bottommost frame in place and secure it with screws to the two 2 × 4s. Hold the other 2 × 4s (the front legs of the unit) in place, one at a time, and secure them, even with the front edge of the frame. (This part of the assembly goes much quicker if you have someone available to help hold the 2 × 4s in place while you set the screws.)

9. Once the top and bottom frames are in place, screw in the other frame units at the 10-inch (25 cm) intervals you've marked on the 2 × 4s.

10. Add two of the 3-foot (91 cm) braces at an angle across the upper sides of the unit. Add two more, angled the opposite direction, across the bottom side of the unit. Secure the final two braces in an upside down "V" on the back of the unit, starting at the top and ending at the sides.

11. Add the casters on the bottom of the legs. The construction work is complete.

12. Slide the tray into place. Add shavings, water bottles, food—and the hamsters.

If you modify this rack, with 20 inches (76 cm) or so larger spaces between the frames, you can place hamster cages directly on top of the frames and not use kitty litter trays. The taller cages would permit you to add exercise wheels to the cages and to provide more stimulation to the hamsters' world.

You can enrich your hamster's cage yourself, or let your pet store provide the goodies.

Cage Enrichment

Cage enrichment is a fairly new term to describe any accessory added to the cage beyond a sleeping tube, food, and water. You'd certainly be bored if you were confined to a single room with nothing to do, and hamsters are really not the stay-at-home type. One group of people who actively seek cage enrichment is zookeepers; they use the World Wide Web on a regular basis to exchange ideas. Zookeepers are extremely innovative in finding ways to enrich enclosures.

Simply because of the difference of scale, it's easier to enhance a hamster's cage than a polar bear's cage or a great ape enclosure. Is the work worth it? You bet. I easily found a dozen or so recent scientific journal articles about hamster cage enrichment and the benefits thereof. Those benefits include reduced aggression, better scores on problem-solving tests, and less fear.

Researchers have very modest ideas of what enriches a cage. One used clear mason jars and sections of PVC pipes, offered one at a time in the caging, to judge reactions more accurately (and I suppose to keep the hammies from getting too excited about their new caging arrangements). The research noted, with a faint air of surprise, that the hamsters were innovative in their use of their enrichment items: they stood on top of the jars and pipes, gnawed on them, urinated in them, and stored food in them. Juveniles slept

You can buy compressed cotton in sheets, to be fluffed by hamsters for bedding.

together in them. The researchers reported that the hamsters in the control cage—without any enrichment—spent more time sleeping and eating than hamsters in the enriched cages. Enrichment seemed to increase species-specific behavior such as scent marking, gnawing, hoarding, and digging. Older hamsters interacted with the enrichment objects less than the younger hamsters, and the enrichment items decreased the aggression in the younger hamsters more than in older hamsters.

In case you're considering which excitement to add to your own cages, the hamsters preferred the jars over the PVC pipes.

But you have many resources at your disposal. If you walk by the hamster or bird section at your local pet store, you'll see devices galore— levered food dispensing containers, plastic balls with jingle bells inside, chew blocks, chew tubes, carrot holders, dyed wooden toys, hanging chains with balls, bells and dowel pieces attached—the variety is limitless. Certainly you can buy whatever you think will appeal to your hamster; none of these items are particularly expensive. The added good news is that you can also provide a lot of stimulation for your hamster with items you find around your house.

Sand

You can use a box of sand. I "cooked" sand in my oven for an hour at 350°F (180°C), in order to kill anything pathogenic. (My husband saw the oven was on, opened the door, and saw a glass dish heaped with sand. He looked puzzled, but said nothing. He did say, "Let's go out for dinner" that night, so this might be worth trying again.)

Once the sand cooled, I poured it into an empty tissue box—the half-sized box—and put it in the cage. The hamsters loved it. I never saw

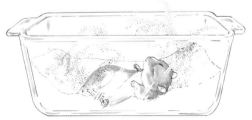

Hamsters enjoy playing and rolling in sand.

them actually roll or dig in it, but within a day they'd shoved most of the sand out of the box and had moved bedding in.

Other Suggestions
• Add an empty soup can.
• Hook together a half-dozen regular paper clips.
• Give them sections of apple or orange branches to gnaw on.
• Cut paper strips and use a glue stick to make a small paper chain.

Whatever route you take, remember to change the items in your hamster's cage every other week or so, just to provide a bit of variety.

Additional Enrichments
• Pieces of fresh coconut
• Plain popped popcorn
• Cardboard tubes from paper toweling or toilet paper
• Pieces of scrap lumber (only untreated lumber); scent some with vanilla or peppermint extract, dot others with food coloring
• Nylabones (you can recycle those your dog has chewed down to nubs too small for him; wash and offer to your hammies)
• Branch sections from fruit trees
• Big (4-inch-long [10 cm]) paper clips, hung from the top of the cage so they swing when touched
• The tiny plastic cups that powdered diet drinks come in
• Extra house keys, washed and strung together with a plastic cable tie

Dealing with an Escapee

Although I like to think my own cages were escape-proof, I was proven wrong—yes, I remembered Israel Aharoni every time. One hamster scrambled on top of his watering bottle and out the top of his uncovered cage. The other hamster shoved open the door of his converted bird cage. Neither escape was a success. The first hamster fell straight down into the bucket I used when changing cages (fortunately the bucket had 4 inches [10 cm] of fresh pine mulch, so the hamster was fine if a bit disappointed when I found him the next morning). The other hamster darted past one of my hound dogs, whose gazelle-like vertical leap told me what was afoot; I was able to reassure my dog that the hamster was no threat to his safety, once I pulled 50 pounds (33 kg) of quivering hound off my shoulders. I retrieved the hamster, who was totally unafraid and more interested in watching the dog than keeping his freedom. I put him back in his cage and added a clip to the door.

But most hamster owners aren't that lucky. They find the cage door open and the hamster is nowhere in sight. You can look for it—you can move the furniture around, noting at the same time the quantities of dust bunnies that live underneath and behind furniture—but you may not see it. Or if you do, you may not be able to grab it before it dashes off.

One friend's hamster found her way into a bathroom and set up her new home underneath the floor of the sink cupboard. My sister's hamster found happiness underneath a refrigerator. Still another hamster crawled up, inside a sofa. All the hiding places offered space, darkness, and privacy.

Traps

You may be able to borrow a rodent live trap from your humane society or your local animal shelter. These are rectangular wire boxes with trip doors that close when the food on the trip tray inside is disturbed. You may be able to rig your own live trap, with the old bucket-and-food trick: You stand the highest bucket (or trash can) in the middle of the floor, and put a few tissues for padding and something

A paper towel tube can be chewed up, slept in, or used as a bolster.

To lure an escaped hamster back into captivity, all you need is a stack of books, a bucket, and some good smelling food.

yummy and smelly in the bottom, perhaps hamster seed mix, some apple pieces, and a little peanut butter. Add a staircase of books to the top of the bucket on one side. Turn off the lights, leave the room, and go to bed. With luck the next morning (or maybe the morning after that), you look inside the bucket and there is your hamster, surrounded by shredded tissues and wearing a guilty look and traces of peanut butter around its mouth.

Hamster-proofing

Hamsters can become family pets, and can be allowed to wander the house when you're home, but with a few restrictions. If you decided you want to give lil' Hammie the freedom to roam around a particular room, hamster-proof the room. Put any dogs or cats in another room and close that door, plug up the tempting holes that are hamster-sized, cover the electric cords, and move any wooden or papier mâché sculptures you may have resting on the floor. Hamsters taste things to help identify them—if the item in question is food, that's good; if not, the hamster moves on.

I hamster-proofed the room I use for an office. For me, this simply meant taking the stuff off the floor of the closet and putting it on the shelves. I moved all the furniture—the file cabinets, the computer desk, the table—about 4 inches (10 cm) away from the wall so Hammie could get behind them and I could peer around *them* to see *him*. After I moved the furniture out, I hastily vacuumed, so Hammie wouldn't get dusty wandering around. Since there are no foodstuffs in the room, well, none that aren't eaten immediately, I didn't have to hamster-proof any food containers, if indeed it's possible to protect foodstuffs against a determined set of gnawing teeth. I moved heavy books from the bottom shelf of my printer stand to a higher shelf, so Hammie couldn't get squashed by a large tome. I covered some electrical cords with split lengths of half-inch (13 mm) aquarium tubing (about a dollar a foot at your aquarium store), and sprayed the others with Bitter Apple, to discourage nibbling. Lastly, I told my entire family that Hammie had roaming privileges in my room and for them to watch their feet when they came into the room.

Once the room was ready, I waited until evening. I put Hammie's cage on the floor, surrounded the area in front of the doorway with assorted hamster toys, and opened the door. It took him a while to get his entire body out of the cage doorway. (I'm sure my room seemed very large to a creature accustomed to the confines of his cage.) But Hammie did venture forth and run behind a file cabinet. It took him the better part of a week of daily forays before he seemed eager to come out and explore when I opened the cage door. Getting him back inside his cage took some time. It took bribery (a raisin trail, leading to the cage) and a bit of herding to get him back in his cage.

He's allowed out only while I'm there, but he's busy while he's out. Because he took an inordinate interest in the carpet in one corner of the room, I had to cover the spot with books to get him to stop trying to dig down through it. Once a week or so, I remove the stash of seeds and nuts he's placed under the printer stand.

Hammie does seem to enjoy his time out of the cage, and he peers at me from around corners as I work. Of course, I'll make certain that Hammie is caged when my office becomes the guest room.

Hamsters and Other Pets

Sometimes it's surprising to see who will live with whom. None of my dogs even blinked an eye when I moved a house rabbit into the front room, although the Pekinese spent the better part of a month asking him to play with her. When I showed Maudie, my yellow-black Syrian (see page 79 to find out more about this color) to my Labrador retriever, I thought the Lab was going to inhale my hands along with the hamster, she was so enchanted. When she punched my hand with her nose so hard I almost dropped Maudie, I realized her enchantment was less than platonic. I worked on developing tolerance in my dogs, but found it difficult when the object of their affections was just mouth-sized and a bit squirmy. Maudie doesn't seem to mind being held and being shown to the dogs, but being sniffed by a much larger beast has to be stressful. I don't think other hamsters would view the process as anything but very stressful. Everyone seems happiest when the hamster is safely behind bars.

Maudie meets dog nose (lower right), under supervision.

Chapter Five

Diet

Hamsters, like a great many if not most other small rodents, are often thought to be strict herbivores. This is not the case at all. Although hamsters do feed predominantly on seed, fruits, and greens, they also opportunistically eat burrowing insects. There has to be some compensation for digging in the dirt, and if that compensation is a bit of a snack, I say, go for it—if you're a hamster, that is. Hamsters may also sample carrion if they come across it.

Hamsters enjoy catching and eating insects.

Despite this somewhat broader than recognized natural diet, pet hamsters of all types are among the easiest small animals to feed, There are a great many commercial diets available, or you can make your own if you wish to do so. Actually, the easiest thing to do is to buy the best-prepared hamster food you can find and augment it with bits and pieces of fresh fruits, fresh veggies, and even an occasional mealworm or cricket or two.

Types of Food

Chow

The hamster foods fall roughly into two types, with an addendum. One type is the chow diet, where all the ingredients are ground up, mixed together, and compacted into uniform brown squares with all the visual appeal of cardboard. Although this diet doesn't look very good to humans, it is a complete diet and provides gnawing exercise for your hamster as well. Chows, also called pelleted foods, when the food is extruded in smaller squares, can truthfully be said to be a better diet because your hamster can't pick and choose what it eats. It will probably come as no surprise to you that many animals want to eat foods that they like, not just foods that are good for them. Hamsters do it, and so do cows.

Mixed Seeds and Grains

The other type of hamster food consists of mixed seeds and ground grains. The mixed seed manufacturers' slant on mixed seed diets is that they are better for hamsters than chows, because the mixed seed diets provide activity opportunities; hamsters will snoop around in their dish of mixed seeds. This is in effect "foraging," just as a hamster would do in the wild, without, of course, the long walks between seeds. The hamster that finds in the wild what's put into seed mixes is one lucky hamster. One is tempted to say, on reading the ingredient list, "Oh, I could live on that. It's just a fortified type of loose granola." One mix includes, in addition to the usual list, almonds, dehydrated apple, and dried carrots, banana, and papaya. No wonder most hamster owners prefer the seed mixes!

Dietary Addenda

The dietary addendum is one most people won't think of, and that's hay, either timothy or alfalfa, or a mix of the two. Hamsters in the wild are grass eaters; they eat it in the field and they pack it into their

Mealworms can be purchased at most pet stores.

cheeks and they take it home and stash it in their larders until winter comes. It's easy to add this component to your hamster's diet, either by buying hay or by pulling fresh grass, if you have access to grass that you know hasn't been treated with a pesticide or herbicide.

Whether or not your hamster will eat it, depends on the hamster. My Chinese hamster woke up, moved out of his exercise wheel/bed to cautiously sniff the grass, seemed to shrug, and went back to bed. My Syrian hamster grabbed the grass and began nibbling. The winter whites were indifferent. I add a twist of timothy to my hamsters' cages every time I change them. Although my hamsters don't leap upon it, they nonetheless nibble on the twist in odd moments. You can buy packaged hay, either in bread loaf-sized bags or compressed into brownie-sized cubes, at your pet store.

Dried timothy hay is good for your hamster—if it will eat it.

Reading Labels

Your hamster has no choice about its diet. It eats what you put in the cage, so it's important for you to know what's in the food you're providing. No matter which diet you decide to offer your pet, read the label before you buy. Some diets, both the pellet and the seed mixes, have added a sweetener to the food. I was surprised to find that I was feeding my hamsters cane molasses with every scoop of seed mix I put into the cages, although molasses is used in many horse feeds.

Freshness

While you're reading labels, check to see if the food should be refrigerated once it's been opened; some brands will advise this. Even if the food doesn't have to be chilled, buy in quantities that you'll use up

within three months or so. You want to feed your hamster food you know is fairly fresh, and if you've ever opened a container of bird seed that's been on your shelf for some time and found that tiny moths have emerged from the mix, you'll know that "fresh" includes the concept

If buying and feeding crickets bothers you, try the cricket and calcium supplements.

"bug-free." There is some thought that the higher oil content of some diets could cause them to go rancid if not refrigerated. Although I've never had any hamster food go rancid because it was too old, I've never had any on hand for more than three months. (One particularly short-lived bag of hamster food delighted my dogs when they nosed the cover of the container off and were industriously lapping the seed mix when I found them. They seemed to enjoy the food, and I'll bet the molasses enhancement was a factor.)

Hamsters usually enjoy all the commercial mixes.

Nutrition

Labels will tell you what's in a food, but they don't tell you much about what a hamster's nutritional needs are. Provide your hamster with a diet that's 12–15 percent protein and 3–6 percent fat. These are quite adequate for nonbreeding animals.

A pregnant or nursing female is going to need a diet that's higher in protein and fat, and an unending supply of water. The same sort of needs apply to the young, once they begin nibbling on solid foods. The young have just over a month to complete body development and become sexually mature. (You have the same amount of time either to find homes for the young or to find extra caging, to separate the sexes.)

Experiments have proven that young hamsters show the most rapid weight gain when provided with a diet that's 18 percent protein, although I would hesitate to use "the heavier the better" as the only criteria when evaluating the development of young animals. We're not yet at the point where we can measure body fat versus mass on hamsters, as we can with people.

Nursing females need a diet that's 15–17% protein.

A winter white displays the three side scallop markings as it waits for a peanut treat.

Treats for Your Hamster Straight from Your Pantry

Offer once or twice a week:
• Eggs—scrambled or hard-boiled (but no salt!)
• Dog biscuits—high in protein and the hard texture will keep the hamster busy (and his teeth worn down)
• Milk—just a teaspoon or less, in a hard-to-turn-over dish
• Mixed bird seeds—your hamster would like parakeet or canary mix
• Nutritional yeast—the sort found in health food stores or sold in a tablet form as a food supplement for dogs and cats. Offer only a half-tablet once a week, and buy those without garlic.
• Dry sugar-free cereal
• Whole wheat bread
• Uncooked pasta

During the breeding season, the diet of the female needs to include a higher percentage of protein. The normal hamster diet has only 12–16 percent protein, so add lab rodent blocks or a few mealworms to the female's food area. For breeding animals, look for a diet that has 15–17 percent protein and 7–9 percent fat. If the mix has a fat content that is higher than 7 percent, use that mix as a treat, or combine it with another food that's lower in fat. One commercial lab block has a protein level of 22 percent, and a fat level of 5 percent; if you use this, add a bit of fat to the diet, such as sunflower seeds.

Vitamins

When you discuss food, you can't help but get into a discussion about vitamin supplements. Most adult humans take vitamins, as a preventive measure. Commercial hamster diets are complete diets, we are told, but at the same time those same food manufacturers produce and sell vitamin supplements. What's going on?

Look upon a vitamin supplement as a form of insurance. Few hamsters gobble up every different type of seed put in their cage. The diet provided may be a good one, but what gets eaten may not be balanced, unless you feed hamster chow. Like humans, hamsters and hamster strains differ from each other genetically. Some strains are very susceptible to maladies such as diabetes or dental caries, which makes them ideal for research on these conditions. It is possible that a vitamin supplement can make the difference between a hamster that gets sick and one that doesn't. Since the vitamins are in a liquid form, designed to be added to the food or to the water in the water bottle, if you're worried about your hamster refusing to eat or drink because it doesn't like the way the vitamins taste, you may want to add a second water bottle, and put the drops only in that bottle.

Mineral Requirements

Interestingly enough, researchers admit that even after all these years, not much is known about the mineral requirements of hamsters. Nonetheless, there are mineral supplements for hamsters on the market. One of the newer items is a calcium tablet that's flavored with cricket bits. That may sound ghoulish, but if you've ever offered your hamster a live cricket, you've seen her make a fool of herself, leaping upon and crunching down the insect before you finish saying, "I don't think she's going to eat that, ohhhhhh, *yuck*." These supplements give your hamster calcium, a necessary mineral, with the tantalizing taste of actual crickets. And you don't have to look at, buy, chase down, or hold a single insect.

Amount to Feed

How much can your hamster eat? A Syrian needs, on the average, about a tablespoon of food a day, plus a few supplements such as bits

Fresh Foods for Your Hamster

Acorns
Apples
Banana
Green beans
Broccoli
Cabbage
Carrots
Cauliflower
Celery
Corn
Zucchini
Cucumbers
Dandelions (leaves and flowers)
Grapes
Kale
Oranges
Peas
Spinach
Sweet potato
Turnip
Watercress

These fresh vegetables are good for your hamster.

of carrot, apple, or a stalk of celery. Offer the same amount to a Chinese, a Campbell's, a winter white or Roborovski, because these hamsters

Syrians will eat out of a food dish, but they will soon move most of the food to the bedroom.

Make your Own Mix

C. H. Keeling, a hamster fancier and keeper in England, makes his own hamster diet from bran, crushed oats, and soya meal, to which he stirs in a standard hamster mix that contains bits of rat blocks, sunflower seeds, dried corn, pea meal, corn flakes, dried peas, and wild bird seed. Keeling adds fresh foods to this admittedly dry diet, varying among apple slices, carrots, and cabbage, which his hamsters only nibble on. His Chinese hamster families enjoy as a group (or may choose to ignore) grass, dandelions, cherries, grapes, and peas. It does sound like a lot of work.

The big pitfall with creating your own food is that unless you work at the numbers for protein, fat, fiber, mineral, and vitamin content, you're feeding your hamster food that may not provide what it needs. I found it easier to read and compare labels and buy the commercial mixes.

seem to have a higher metabolism than the Syrians. When you first put the seed mix into the food, your hamster may glean out what it likes best—and who can blame your pet? Some mixes include dried papaya, bananas, raisins, peanuts, almonds, admittedly not quite what a hamster would find in the wild. So they eat more on the first day than they will on the third.

Fresh Foods

Fresh foods can include almost any sort of fruit or vegetable. The only one you need to be wary of would be the leafy greens, such as romaine or spinach; however, giving a piece bigger than an inch square can cause temporary diarrhea.

Snacks

You might be amazed at the variety and number of hamster snacks available for you and your hammie. Use them, of course, but cautiously, because they aren't complete diets. Most of them are very appealingly packaged, using bright colors such as red, which is an appetite stimulant in humans. Some of them look so much like human food that I won't tell anyone if you don't. Most of the commercial treats contain sweeteners such as sugar, honey, or corn sugar, and are brightly colored themselves. I was curious about some snacks that look like brightly colored sticks, and tasted them myself. They were sweet, so I checked the label. The main ingredients were flour and corn syrup, not much to offer, nutrition-wise. Hamsters will willingly eat more sweet treats than a balanced diet, so you'll have to limit the treats offered.

Snack products fall into two basic groups—the mixes and the single-item foods. The mixes combine such things as peanuts, molasses, papaya, apples, carrots, and sunflower seeds, usually compressed into nuggets large enough for a human to easily handle.

The single-food treats are generally dried fruits or vegetables. The small ears of dried corn look like they'd be fun as well as providing hours of disassembly time. Another manufacturer offers dried mango, papaya, banana, and pineapple. Compare the ones you can buy at your pet store, which in many cases are produced overseas, with the dried fruits you can buy at your local health food store. The pet items are packed in 50-gram packages for about a dollar a package, which computes to about 66 cents an ounce. Dried mangoes for human consumption cost about the same at my local health food store.

Are these snacks necessary? No, not at all; even though you may enjoy

There's a world of hamster treats to select from; just offer them in moderation.

feeding your pet something you know it likes, you need to provide proper nutrition.

When You Leave Home

The ability to store food is one reason why you can leave your hamster for three or four days without worrying. Give it fresh water, make certain the cage has just been cleaned, and check the seed/food supply (and top it off, if needed). If you're worried about sudden temperature changes in your house or apartment, the cage is a self-contained unit that can be handed to a friend or neighbor.

Chapter Six

Selecting Your Hamster

Hamsters as Pets

Hamsters are rodents with an acute sense of smell. They love to explore their surroundings, they are curious about everything, and if you give them a minute to wake up, they don't even mind awakening out of a deep snooze to visit with you. They interact with each other, and can identify each other by scent. They will shred up paper towels, explore their cage, check out what's new in the food dish, and run in their wheel for hours at a time. They are always interested in their surroundings and if they could just juggle that cage door open a bit, they'd check out *your* surroundings as well.

If watching and handling a live-wire, good-natured pocket-sized pet seems like fun to you, a hamster is a good choice. But you also need to know that hamsters are not animals you can handle and pet for long periods of time, like a dog. They will not crawl over the arms and shoulders of a complete stranger like a fur-covered Slinky, or decide to explore your bed and mock-attack you, as would a ferret. They won't approach you and expect to be petted, briefly, and

then stalk away, as does a cat. They won't hop over to your breakfast plate and nibble on your toast, as would a parakeet. If these "won'ts" sound like advantages to you, you're a hamster person.

Hamsters will sit in your hands for a few minutes, and if you let your hamster get to know you, it will even fall asleep in your hands. But then it would like to get back in its cage, to familiar surroundings.

Costs

Like everything else, pet hamsters cost money, although they're certainly not as expensive as a dog or a cat; they're a lot less fussy about eating than cats, too!

Here's how to budget hamster ownership—and these are minimal costs.

The first year you'll spend about $155:
• Caging—A 10-gallon (38-L) aquarium costs about $20; the top is another $10
• The animal will cost about $10
• Food will be about $50
• Veterinarian visits will be about $50. You should budget this amount because your hamster can seem to

Hamsters are good-natured pets that enjoy interacting with their owners.

be extremely healthy one moment and the next is lying on its side outside its sleeping area and panting. When you need a veterinarian, you *need* a veterinarian.

• Additional toys, accessories, chew treats, exercise balls will run at least $15.

Total: $155. Less than a single-car payment, the price of one nice dinner out for two people, or an all-right meal for four. You have instead a charming companion that enjoys exploring your pockets and taking sunflower seeds from your fingers. It won't borrow money from you and forget to repay it. It won't take the last cup of coffee from your pot and not start a new pot. What a bargain you've made!

Time

Your hamster doesn't need much time, just a half-hour a day spent with you, exploring your pockets, your sleeves, your desktop, or sofa (remember: watch your little Houdini—it can squeeze into the tiniest places and "escape" right before your eyes. One hamster did just that—the family moved during the ensuing year and gave up on their hamster entirely. One day they found it strolling along the top of the sofa, evidently the place it had been for a year. It had been able to filch enough food and find water during all that time.) Hamsters can be smarter than we might think. Don't give yours a chance to upstage you.

What Kind of Hamster to Buy

Do you want a calm hamster, one that will seem to enjoy being held and that will willingly crawl out of its opened cage door and into your hands, even if it's only for a minute or two? Then you'll want a Syrian hamster.

If you want a beautifully marked hamster, one that's small and rounded in shape, but still quick on its feet, you'll want a Campbell's hamster.

If you like the shape of a Campbell's but you like a bit of a change now and then, you may want a winter white, the dwarf hamster that changes from gray to white during the winter, and back to gray in the spring.

If you want a very small hamster that wears its white eyebrow patches as if in perpetual surprise, you'll want a Roborovski hamster.

A long-haired black-eyed cream Syrian "show" hamster.

This is a very quick hamster that some breeders appreciate. Mine were ready to nip any intruding hand, and it took me some weeks before they stopped nipping. Their agility in wiggling out of my hands made me feel like I was trying to hold live Jell-O.

If you want to keep more than one hamster, and don't want to set up separate cages for each individual, you'll want one of the communal hamsters, the Roborovskis, the Chinese, the Campbell's, or the winter whites. These live well in small groups, particularly if they've been brought up together, although you may hear some squeaked discussions at night.

Sexes: Don't forget that if you have both sexes, sooner or later you'll end up with babies; the winter pause for breeding tends to be disrupted if you use artificial lights and turn what had been short days into long days. But if they do have young, you'll have a chance to watch something that has only recently been noted—male-female pairs of Campbell's and winter whites sharing in the care of the young (see pages 21 and 24 for more on parental care).

Hair: If you like the idea of a long-haired hamster, then one of the long-haired Syrians may be the pet for you. You may end up actually trimming the coat if it catches up too much litter or shavings; brushing or combing tends to pull out the hair rather than removing the tangles. You'll really notice this if the hamster is a male; the males' coats are longer than those of the females.

This lilac male Syrian has a good "chunky" body but not a good long coat.

How to Choose

So you've done a bit of research, and you're pretty certain you want a Syrian, one as close to the standard golden color as you can find. But there are four Syrians in the cages in front of you. How do you know which one to pick?

You need to hold your potential hamster, even for just a minute or two. Ask the pet store employee or the breeder to take it out of the cage for you, or if you feel you can maneuver the hamster out of its cage (some of those door openings are small!), pick it up yourself. If you're taking the hamster out of the cage, try to scoop it up in your hand from behind, or put a small dish in the cage and shoo it into the dish.

There are three ways to pick up a hamster.

1. The one most useful and easiest to do uses both hands. You shoo the hamster onto one hand with the other and cup your hand over the hamster, using your fingers to form a cage around the hamster. Compress your hands slightly so both palms can feel the hamster, and move your fingers so it can't squeeze through them.

2. The second method is the nape hold. You put your hand over the hamster, pinning it against the substrate, and use your thumb and forefinger to grasp the nape of its neck. Lift the hamster, and let its body slide down inside its skin, a little like a golfball inside a sock. This hold takes practice, although it does immobilize the hamster so you can sex him or her. My hamsters didn't seem to like this hold, so I use it only when necessary.

A male long-hair Syrian explores the hands that hold it.

Hold your hamster in your cupped hands.

3. The third hold is another one-hand hold. You place your hand over the hamster, but with its head pointing toward your wrist. Your forefinger and middle finger are on each side of its rump, and your thumb and ring finger grasp it under the armpits. This puts the head at the base of your hand. When you turn your hand over, flex your wrist so your fingers point toward the

The nape hold; none of my hamsters liked it.

floor. This puts the hamster on its back, in the palm of your hand.

Once you have the hamster in hand, see how it responds to you. Does it seem to enjoy being held, perhaps after a few moments of trying to get through your fingers? Does it nestle into your hand and then look upward toward your face?

Don't discount one automatically because it flops over onto its back and bares its teeth as your hand approaches. Give that hamster a few minutes to calm down and try again, making certain that this time you wash your hands so you don't bring in any possible odors from another hamster.

Look at and hold at least three, so you'll know you picked the best one when you take your new pet home. I'd advise against buying one that nips you. Of course, you can probably tame it, but you can also buy a hamster that doesn't nip from the start.

If the pet store doesn't want you to hold their hamsters prior to selecting

Syrian littermates display partial and full banding.

one to purchase, try another pet store. You and your hamster will be together for the rest of its life, and you need one that you'll enjoy owning and handling.

Picking a Healthy Hamster

The basic rules for picking a healthy hamster are the same as any other mammal. No matter what species you select, look for one with bright eyes and an inquisitive attitude. Unless you're buying an alien hamster— the hairless morph of the Syrians—look for a hamster with a full, even coat. When you hold it, take a moment to run your fingers lightly over the shoulder and hips. Although cancers are rare in hamsters, they do occur. I was selecting hamsters to take to our local pet store for resale and picked up our best yellow-blacks, a Syrian that has a black overcoat and a tawny yellow undercoat. There was a lump on her shoulder—a tumor. We kept her, of course, but it was by chance that I felt the tumor. I don't think our pet store would have picked up on the problem, and perhaps not even the new owner, unless that owner had had the sense to pick up and lightly inspect his or her potential hamster pet.

Dominant spot (left) and normal (right) Chinese hamsters.

Black Syrian hamsters have white feet and gray ears.

Does Age Matter?

Any species of hamster you buy has an expected lifespan of 18 months to two years. (Roborovskis may live three years.) As a parent, you may welcome a pet that won't commit you to years of tending, cleaning, and feeding; of course your kids have agreed to take care of everything their hamster might need every minute of the day, but sometimes parents still have to take care of their kids' animals.

If you want to spend every possible moment with your hamster, from weaning through old age (the hamster's, that is), buy a young one. There are very few things cuter than a baby hamster of any kind. Certainly it's easy to get a very young hamster to adapt to you and your household.

If you feel that a year is long enough to spend with a hamster, go

for the adult. If for any reason the adult you get doesn't seem tame, just work with it for a few minutes at least once a day; hamsters can remember some odors from other hamsters for only 24 hours, so don't give yours the chance to "forget" you. I do need to warn you, though: If you think that having a hamster for only a year or so will ease the heartache when it goes to the great hamster wheel in the sky, think again. It would be hard not to fall in love with a small, alert, bright-eyed creature that regards you as a bringer of good things, one that never has to be taken outside, never has to get expensive inoculations, won't make so much noise your neighbors complain, and won't destroy your house while you're away. Having a hamster-sized hole in your heart can be very uncomfortable.

Which Sex?

I don't think it matters which sex you choose, although some people will tell you the females are fiercer. Males, of course, are never pregnant when you buy them, so if you do buy a male you won't be surprised by young a few weeks later. Male and female hamsters both make good companions. Obviously, there are physical differences between the males and females; one of my friends declined the offer of a male Chinese hamster because she didn't like the way he looked (the male Chinese hamsters are the ones with the very noticeable testicles). If you want more than one hamster and you want to keep them together, you'll probably want a same-sex grouping of one of the communal species. Perhaps a female grouping would be more harmonious than a male grouping, although I've kept both types with no problems.

Sources for Hamsters

Where you get your hamster depends to a great degree on how long you've thought about the process. The costs begin at zero and go up from there.

Impulse

Some people acquire their hamster rather as a spur-of-the-moment impulse, or perhaps a spur-of-the-moment weakness, on your own part or on the part of a family member. The classified ads in your local newspaper do occasionally have "hamsters free to a good home" ads, and company bulletin boards are another source of these ads. If you have a child under 12, you probably already know whether your kid is vulnerable to acquiring pets. Kids can be disarming when questioned about the newest animal. Your child may be capable of assuring you he doesn't know *where* he got the hamster with cage setup now sitting in his room.

The impulse hamsters tend to be low-cost or free, and are from a friend of the family or a school chum of any age. Usually the cage and the food/bedding are added as an inducement.

Pet Stores

The next step up in hamster acquisition is the pet store. Hamsters from a pet store are modestly priced, usually between $7 and $15, and the cost of cage/bedding/feeding/dishes/feed tend to be added on to that original animal price. As a special promotion, some pet stores will throw in a hamster when you buy the hamster setup. I personally feel this makes the hamster less valuable. "After all, the hamster didn't cost me anything." The dispassionate bargain attitude toward the hamster is only temporary, until you see how children respond to the personality and shoe-button eyes, and discover what fun this furry little dynamo can be during its waking hours.

You can be fairly certain that the hamster you buy from a pet store will be in good health and good condition. They are usually maintained in one-hamster cages, with little to

Most pet stores stock a variety of hamsters and other rodents.

A hamster breeder is your best choice for something unusual, like this chocolate Campbell's.

no chance of biting each other, spreading diseases, or becoming pregnant.

Some pet stores however, sell hamsters from a communal cage. This shouldn't be cause for concern since hamsters can get along tem-

This is a black mottled Campbell's.

porarily under what we'd consider very crowded (more than three to a cage) conditions. The adults get along in sort of a forced détente, agreeing not to fight for now but willing to change that rule if anyone starts acting up. The mating urge is slowed during the winter months. Young born under crowded cage conditions rarely survive the night (see page 101 for more on this dark side of hamster mothering).

Once hamsters get away from the crowded caging, things may change. Females purchased from a communal cage and given proper housing, good food, and a bit of bedding in a snug corner of their own cage, are more than likely to surprise you with a litter anywhere from a week to two weeks postpurchase. (Remember, even if you hear squeaking, don't bother the mom or her babies. This means stay *away* from the cage for at least a week except to provide food and water.)

The advantage of buying from a pet store is that you're assured that your hamster has been given good food and housing while it has been in the store, and that you'll have some good advice on the sex of your hamster. Usually there's a guarantee that the animal is in good health. This means that the store will at least replace the animal if it dies within 48 hours. This doesn't help the hamster any, but at least you will still have a hamster. If you buy from a pet store, you'll have the help of the staff on what caging and supplies to buy, and you can take everything home with you. The staff earnestly hopes you will enjoy your new hamster, and that you'll return to the store soon for some of those eye-catching accessories and play gear, a few packets of hamster treats, and perhaps another, larger cage.

Hamster Shows/Breeders

If you're very lucky, you'll be able to attend a hamster show, or find a professional breeder near you, or if you don't mind waiting a day or so and live near an airport, you can have your hamster shipped to you, but few beginner hamster keepers want to go to that much trouble. A breeder is a treasure several times over. He or she (most of the professional breeders I know are female, but there are certainly males out there) knows hamsters like no one you've ever met. Professional breeders keep records, generation after generation, of records. They know what lines ought not to breed with what lines (see page 95 in the breeding chapter as to why this is important), they know what colors are popular and what shades are new, they know the latest on commercial hamster foods and will gladly tell you what they use and why, they have hamsters of different ages, so you can buy an adult if you want an adult, or you can buy a weanling if you want a young hamster. They know where and when the next show will be held, so even if you only want to go see a show to see if hamster breeders are as *feverish* about their hobby as are the orchid

breeders. (But be warned—being tempted is part of going to a show—see Chapter Nine for more about shows.) The best thing about the professional breeders is that they really like hamsters, they really care for and about their hamsters, and they've bred their lines for specific qualities.

I can see you gingerly feeling in the direction of your wallet, and asking, "But aren't those professionals a lot more expensive than pet stores?" They aren't appreciably more expensive, at least not for a pet hamster. Like show dogs, not every hamster in a litter is a show-quality hamster, and those less-than show-quality hamsters are what the breeder is happy to sell to individuals and to pet stores. Instead of buying a hamster that really looks pretty much like every other hamster you've seen from a pet store, you'll have a hamster from a known lineage, from a hamster breeder who

Campbell's soon lose any fear of being handled.

takes pride in breeding for temperament *and* show-quality coat/color/conformation—a terrific bargain for you—and for the lucky hamster you take home.

Retired Hamsters

You may be able to get a retired hamster, a former breeder. This is a new program, and one of the first hamster groups to initiate it is the Diamond State Hamster Fanciers Association. Some hamster breeds live far longer than their breeding effectiveness; Syrians have a useful breeding life of one year, and generally can live a year and a half beyond that. The Association distributes hamster vouchers through pet stores in the Delaware Valley area. Someone who purchases a hamster cage gets a voucher, and can call the contact person listed on the voucher. They agree on a date and a time for that person to look at the retired breeders available and to choose one to adopt. The usual

adoption fee is waived. The goal is to also place unwanted, rescued hamsters via this technique as well.

Sexing Hamsters

Some hamster species are very easy to sex—you can look at Chinese rat-tailed hamsters and sex them; the males have very large testicles. The other hamster types need to be held to be sexed.

The Syrians, the Campbell's, and the Roborovskis should be grasped gently but firmly around the body and lifted. Hamsters don't like being held almost upright, leaning back a tad, so the hamster will struggle. Hold fast. If it wriggles too much for you to be comfortable, you can try the famous nape hold (see page 78), which got me bitten the two times I tried it. This is the hold that researchers use, and they've gotten good at it. You want to pick up the hamster by the nape of its neck, but

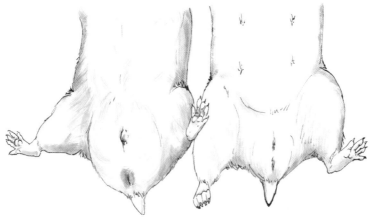

Hamsters don't need any help in determining the sex of each other, but you might. The male hamster is on the left, the female on the right.

Go ahead. Open the cage door and wait for a minute or so.

pull that skin away from the body and use your other fingers to keep the skin at the nape of the neck—the skin held in your fingers—taut. Your hamster will essentially slide down inside that loose skin and be stuck until you turn it loose. I found it easier to put my fingers under the hamster's armpits, lift it up, and to support the fat little body with my other hand.

When you have your hamster immobilized, look at the genital area, the lower belly where the tail meets the body. Female hamsters have the genital opening and the anus close together, perhaps a ¼ inch (6 mm) or so apart, one right above the other. Males have the genital opening separated from the anal opening by a distance about equal to the width of your forefinger. And in males older than five weeks, when you hold him upright, the testes fall down to the edge of the body, forming two dis-

tinct pale pink lumps on each side of the anus.

Taming Your Hamster

So there it is, in its cage. And there you are, looking at your hamster, knowing you ought to pick it up and begin taming it because you don't want to get bitten and you sure don't want your kids to be bitten. But—is it tame?

In a word, yes. Hamsters are nice creatures, even when new captives. Mike Murphy, the graduate student who brought new Syrian stock back from Aleppo in 1971, was amazed at how quickly the hamsters he and his wife captured tamed down.

The 1930s descendents have been bred for disposition for many years. Breeders and researchers don't like getting bitten anymore

A frightened hamster may flop over onto its back and play dead.

than you and I do. You can do the math: Hamsters are ready to breed at two months, and about every month after that. Under artificial lighting, they can breed all year-round, so you could have seven generations a year, allowing for some time off for good (or "bad" depending on how you look at it) behavior. So that's seven litters a year, figuring in replacement parents every eighteen months. This happens for 70 years if we're talking about Syrians, so that's 490 successive generations of hamsters. Hamsters—all of them—have been and are being bred for disposition. Even Syrians, supposedly the solitary hamsters, have been bred by at least one lab to get along with each other—wow! All you need is a bit of your time to work with your hamster, so it will know you aren't bad news.

So stop worrying. Wash your hands, and dry them. Open the cage and look at your hamster.

• If it's sleeping, rustle the substrate near it until it wakes up, or very gently jiggle the cage. Hamsters don't like to be awakened suddenly, because it might mean something is going to eat them. It's much like having your kid prying open your eyelids early on a Saturday morning and announcing "some guys at the door say they are from the IRS. They say they want to talk to you." That's not a good way to wake up.

• Waking up needs to be a pleasant experience for all concerned, so always give your hamster a moment to wake up. It needs to open its shoe-button eyes and focus on your earnest face. Once it's looking at you, reach in and scoop it up in your fingers (from the rump side first is best). Close your fingers around it. As soon as you get your hand off the substrate, cup your other hand over it to make a cage of your fingers. Your hamster can look out but can't get out. In effect, you're cupping your hamster within your hands.

• Talk to it while you do this. Of course, it won't be able to understand your words, but it will be able to pick up on the tone you use.

• Hold it closely so it can't escape, or cup it against your body. Your hamster needs to feel secure—that it's not going to be dropped. You don't want to drop it, ever, because you don't want to hurt it and you don't want to play "find the hamster" late at night.

But what if your hamster sees you coming, rolls over on its back, bares its teeth, and squeaks? Back off a minute. The little fellow is scared and is trying to fend off what it sees as your attack. Relax, and let your pet roll over and compose itself. Talk to it. In a few minutes try again, but this time, scoop it up in an empty tin can, or if it has sought shelter in an empty paper towel roll, pick up the roll and cover both ends. Uncover the lower end and tip the hamster out into your hand. Hold it close to your body. Chances are, it's frightened. Put yourself in your hamster's place.

• Once you have your hamster in your hands, and it has settled down a bit, spend a few minutes talking to it and stroking its head or back gently. Offer a sunflower seed or a raisin (raisin bread is a fine source of an occasional raisin). Your hamster will enjoy this once it gets over being frightened, but it will take several sessions before it figures out that you're a friend and not an enemy.

If you can handle your hamster a half-dozen times over a weekend, or a couple of times a day for four or five days, it will look forward to being out of the cage with you.

What Color Is My Hamster?

Thanks to the patience and skill of breeders, hamsters come in far more colors than the basic brown gold of the Syrians and the brown gray of the Campbell's. They now are available in several coat textures and patterns that are independent of the colors.

You can basically pick a color, a pattern, and a coat texture, and find a Syrian or a Campbell's to match. The winter whites, Roborovski, and Chinese hamsters have far fewer colors and coats to select from.

Exercising even more skill, the breeders have a name and a description for every color, pattern, and coat morph. To see what sort of hamster you probably have, pick up your hamster and thumb through this list, which is derived from Lorraine Hill. There is room for discussion here, though. Breeders tend to form their own definition of some of the colors, and unless you know what the parents looked like, you don't know the genetic background of your hamster.

Hint: You'll need to know the color of your hamster's coat. Just because your hamster is an overall pale gray doesn't mean your hamster is pale gray all the way through.

An argente pearl Campbell's hamster.

The original "golden" Syrian color is still popular.

Use your fingers to part your hamster's fur, and notice what color the fur is both next to the skin and at the end of the hair shaft.

Syrians

Colors

Golden: Like the wild form, the fur of the modern golden Syrian is dark gray at the roots and a golden brown at the tips. There is a dark line that extends from the bottom of the face, just under the ears, back over the shoulders, and the "cheek streak." The ears are dark gray, the belly is ivory, and the eyes dark.

Black: The animal is entirely black, with white feet, gray ears, and dark eyes. The fur is black from root to tip. This is the hamster called the "black bear" by some hamster breeders and pet stores.

Brown (dove): The fur is pale brown from the roots to the tips. The belly is ivory. The ears are pale and the eyes are red. The eyes darken with age, but in a flashlight beam are still a burgundy color.

Chocolate: (Now, *this* is a color to love.) There are two shades of chocolate. The sable form has fur that's pale milk chocolate with *paler* roots. The ears are gray and the eyes dark. The black chocolate is a dark chocolate fur from roots to tips. The feet are white. The ears are gray and the eyes are dark.

Cinnamon: The attractive ginger color conceals a blue-gray undercoat. The belly is ivory. The ears are pale and the eyes are red.

Copper: The body fur is a deep copper with darker roots. The fur around the eyes is paler copper, and the ears are pale. The eyes are red. The eyes darken with age, but in a flashlight beam are still a burgundy color.

Cream with black eyes: The fur is cream to the roots. The cream becomes a bit more tan in tone as the animal matures. The ears are gray, and the eyes are dark.

Cream with red eyes: The fur is pink-toned cream from root to tip, and the color intensifies as the animal matures. The ears are pale, and the eyes are red, darkening with age.

Gray (dark): The fur is gray with darker roots. The belly is ivory. The "cheek streak" is black.

Gray (light): Pale gray fur with dark gray roots. The muzzle is almost white and the cheek streak is dark brown-gray. The belly is ivory. The ears are dark and the eyes are black.

Gray (silver): The fur is silvery gray with dark gray roots. The belly is ivory. The ears are dark and the eyes are black.

Ivory with black eyes: The fur is almost but not quite white from root to tip. The ears are gray and the eyes are dark.

Ivory with red eyes: The fur is almost but not quite white from root to tip. The ears are pale. The eyes are red and may darken to burgundy with age.

Lilac: The fur is gray with a lavender tone, which may take on a brown coloration as the animal matures. The roots are gray. The belly is ivory. The ears are pale and the eyes are red.

Pearl (smoke): The fur is pale gray at the root, darkening to black at the tip. The belly is ivory. The ears are gray and the eyes are black.

Rust: Almost a copper color but a bit browner, with gray roots. The ears are gray and the eyes are dark. This color is not yet available in the United States; although some breeders have selectively bred their Syrians for a rustlike color, the color does not breed true because the rust gene is not present.

Sable: The fur is black with cream roots. There are cream circles around the eyes. As the animal matures, the black may fade to brown or dark gray. The eyes are dark.

Sable roan: The fur is white with sable hairs ticked throughout. The ears are pale and the eyes are black.

Tortoiseshell: This hamster is the result of a cross between a yellow and another color. When yellow is bred with black, and the offspring bred with white, you get a hamster that looks like a calico cat, with patches of reddish brown, white, and black. Interestingly enough, most tortoiseshell hamsters are females; the males are very rare, just like the cats.

Umbrous golden: Like the golden hamster, but the golden areas are tinged with gray and the belly is gray.

White with dark ears: The fur is white from root to tip. The ears are dark, and turn even darker as the animal ages. The eyes are red.

White with pale ears: This is the result of a cross between the dark-eared white and the cinnamon. The fur is pure white. The ears are pale and the eyes red.

Hamsters explore with their noses and their eyes.

Syrian hamsters are agile explorers.

Coat Patterns

Banded: This is a combination between a white and any other color. The white is on the belly and in a band across the back. The band may or may not be solid; it may be interrupted by the other color.

Dominant spot: This is white combined with a color to produce a hamster with a white belly and a white-with-color-splotched back. The splotches are most obvious on the side of the body.

Roan: The fur is any color, mixed with a sprinkle of white hairs. The base color is most distinct on the head.

Coat Length

There are four coat types.

Hairless: Also called the alien hamster. There is no fur on the body with the possible exception of whiskers. Alien females often do not produce enough milk to feed their young.

Normal coat: A short coat with no texture.

Yellow: The fur is yellow-tan with dark tips. The black tipping seems to intensify with age. The ears are dark and the eyes are black.

Yellow-black: this is a cross between the yellow and black. The fur is yellow and heavily tipped with black. The feet are paler than the body. The ears are gray and the eyes are dark.

Male tortoiseshell Syrian hamsters are very rare.

These normal-coated banded Syrian babies had banded parents.

Long-haired: This is sometimes called the teddy-bear hamster. The fur is long, sometimes as long as 4 inches (10 cm) in areas. The males have the longer coats.

Rex: The fur curls upward, both in short-haired and long-laired forms. With the short-haired forms, the result is a plush-looking hamster. With the long-haired forms, it's a bit like Einstein and static electricity.

Satin: The hair, although sparse, has a very glossy appearance.

Campbell's

Coat Colors

Normal: The fur is brown-gray, with dark roots. A dark stripe runs from the head to the tail. The belly is white. The ears are gray and the eyes are dark.

Normal, with mottling: The fur is white with patches of brown-gray. The dorsal stripe is dark but may not be complete. The belly is white. The ears are gray and the eyes are dark or red.

Normal, with platinum: The fur is brown-gray with white hairs sprinkled throughout. The ears are pale and the eyes are black.

Albino: The fur is white, from root to tip. There is no dorsal stripe. The ears are pale and the eyes are red.

Argente with red eyes: The fur is reddish brown or cinnamon with blue-gray roots. The dorsal stripe is a muted dark gray. The belly is white. The ears are pale and the eyes are red.

Argente with black eyes: The fur is pale reddish brown or cinnamon with gray roots. The dorsal stripe is dark gray. The belly is

A normal-coated platinum Campbell's hamster.

white. The ears are gray and the eyes are black.

Argente, mottled: The fur is mottled white with cinnamon; the cinnamon portions have blue-gray roots. The dorsal stripe is a muted dark gray and may not be complete. The belly is white. The ears are pale and the eyes are red.

Beige: This is a cross between the argente and the black-eyed argente. The fur is pale orange-beige, and the dorsal stripe is darker. The belly and muzzle are white. The ears are pale and the eyes are red.

Blue fawn: The fur is reddish brown with a blue tint. The roots are blue-gray, as is the dorsal stripe. The belly is ivory. The ears are pale and the eyes are red.

Black: The fur is very dark gray to black, from roots to tips. The dorsal stripe is darker than the fur but barely visible. The feet and chin are white. The ears are gray and the eyes are black.

Black, mottled: The fur is mottled white with patches of dark gray to black. The dorsal stripe is barely visible. The feet and chin are white. The ears are black and white and the eyes are black.

The blue Campbell's has an indistinct dorsal stripe.

Blue: This is a cross between opal and black. The fur is gray-blue, and the dorsal stripe darker but largely indistinct. The ears are gray and the eyes are black.

Blue, mottled: The fur is gray-blue with white patches. The dorsal stripe is darker but largely indistinct. The ears are gray and the eyes are black.

Blue fawn: This is a cross between opal and argente. The fur is blue-tan in color. The dorsal stripe is darker but indistinct. The ears are pale and the eyes are red.

Chocolate: This is a cross between the black-eyed argente and the black. The fur is a medium brown, rather a pale milk chocolate color, with a slightly darker dorsal strip. The eyes are black.

Dove: This is a cross between the black and argente. The fur is gray, with a slightly darker dorsal stripe. The belly is ivory. The ears are pale and the eyes are red. The eyes darken with age, but in a flashlight beam are still a burgundy color.

Dove, mottled: The fur is gray, with white patches. The dorsal stripe is indistinct. The belly is ivory. The ears are pale and the eyes are red. The eyes darken with age, but flash red in a flashlight beam.

Lilac fawn: This is a cross between opal and the black-eyed argente. The fur is blue-tan, and the dorsal stripe is a slightly darker shade. The ears are pale and the eyes are black.

Opal: The fur is blue-gray with ivory belly and muzzle. The sides are tan. The dorsal stripe is slightly

A black-eyed argente Campbell's hamster.

darker. The ears are gray and the eyes are dark.

Opal mottled: The fur is blue-gray with white patches and white belly and muzzle. The dorsal stripe is slightly darker and not distinct. The ears are pale to gray and the eyes are dark.

Opal platinum: The fur is blue-gray with white hairs mixed in. The belly and muzzle are white, but these don't contrast as strongly as in the darker opal. The dorsal stripe is dark but indistinct. The ears are gray and the eyes are dark.

White with black eyes: Also called a dilute platinum. The fur is white, and there is no dorsal stripe. The ears are white and the eyes are dark.

White with red eyes: The fur is white, and there is no dorsal stripe. The ears are white and the eyes are red.

Chapter Seven

Reproduction

About Breeding in General

On the surface, breeding your hamsters looks to be an easy way to make a little money. Pet stores sell the little critters for $5 and up; if each litter contains eight babies, that's $40 if you sell them yourself, $20 if you sell them to the pet store.

It doesn't quite work that way. National chain pet stores avoid penny-ante customer complaints

One is terrific, but what will you do with 12 hamsters?

about livestock by having only a few suppliers for the entire chain. This gives them real leverage if there is something wrong with the animals being supplied, and avoids headaches in trying to find out which backyard hamster breeder Store # 56 bought the male champagne hamsters from. National chains buy from only the breeders on their list, and the buying is centralized. Your local branch can't take your hamsters for a dollar each or even for free.

Local pet stores generally get all they need from their local sources— their daughter's chorus teacher, for instance, or the local stores get their hamsters for free from people who no longer wish to keep their hamsters. Even notices thumbtacked onto bulletin boards don't get much response—or not a response in time for you to move your new babies out before they need separate caging. When I posted such a notice, the only response I got was from a man who had just gotten a pair of hamsters, a male and female, and wanted to know when they'd have babies. When I replied, "Sooner than you might think," he admitted that the female was getting fat. (He called back a few days later and offered me the mother, her ten newly born young, and the father. "The miracle of birth" had proved to be more than he could handle.) Unless you have six people waiting and asking for young from your hamsters, breeding may not turn out the way you hope it will.

Genetic Problems

In case you're wondering if the hamsters you're thinking of breeding may not produce the young you're looking for, talk to a breeder, someone who has already been down the pathway and who can help you avoid making mistakes. There are breeders' web sites filled with information on good pairing and bad pairing combinations. The wrong sort of pairings can produce young with morphological defects or behavioral defects.

In Campbell's hamsters, the mottled gene can present problems. When parents with the ruby-eyed mottled gene (ruby eyes and pinto-like markings) are bred, the young have serious birth defects. If you're wondering if your hamsters have ruby eyes, the eyes reflect red in a flashlight beam although they look dark to your unaided eyes.

When the mottled gene in Campbell's is bred to another mottled Campbell's, the young are smaller and white; very pretty, but evidently

Avoid breeding two mottleds together.

eyeless (anophthalmic) and may be toothless. It's a little hard to tell on the latter, because the babies die when they're two to three weeks old.

In Syrian hamsters the recessive anophthalmic gene is the troublemaker. When heterozygous for the anophthalmic gene, the normal-appearing parents have roan coloring or a white belly. Because they are heterozygous, they have one dominant gene or gene grouping for normal coloration and normal eyes, and a recessive gene/gene grouping for the white color and eyelessness. When two of these hamsters are bred, some of the young receive both recessive genes, and as a result are white (which is why all-white hamsters merit your close examination before you buy them) and eyeless. These babies can muddle around their cages and find food and water, but they don't have much appeal as a pet.

An albino Campbell's can pass on the hidden or recessive mottled gene.

When you find that some colors can "mask" the mottled gene, breeding hamsters of that color can be iffy. An albino Campbell's can mask a mottled gene. If you breed a mottled to a masked albino, you'll have some young that have two recessive genes for mottled. Those babies will be white, and will die within two to three weeks.

Syrian females come into season (estrus) every four days during the summer or short-day cycle.

Behavioral Defects

The behavioral defects are not linked to color or to species of hamster. They seem to be the result of a mutation that is carried on if there is a limited gene pool (which is certainly the story with hamsters!). If these behaviors occurred in humans we'd call them obsessive-compulsive disorders.

Waltzing mice, where the mouse turns in tight circles, are one example of a behavioral trait. Pacing in Campbell's hamsters is another inherited trait. The hamster selects a pathway along one side of the cage, or across the center, or just a few inches this way and a few inches back. It paces back and forth, day after day. It pauses to eat, to drink, to sleep and defecate, but little more. Another form of pacing is lap running, where the pathway extends around the perimeter of the cage. T. Nishio and N. Hayasi reported a spontaneous mutation in a closed colony of Armenian hamsters *(C. migratorius),* which was characterized by speedy, lap-running behavior, a bit unusual because this behavior is not accompanied by any other motor or auditory deficits. For cases where the behavior is constant, the hamsters should be euthanized.

Backflipping in Campbell's is another behavioral extreme. This first appears when the hamster is about five weeks old. The hamster stands, but does a backflip and lands on its feet again. Sometimes it may face a different direction than when it started. This flip seems to be involuntary, not something a hamster does when it wants to or out of joy. It may do this again and again during waking hours. If this is the case, the hamster should be euthanized.

The Facts on Reproduction

Puberty and Mating

Estrus is the period of time, usually about 12 hours long, when the female will mate with the male. Since hamster females come into season, or into estrus, every four days, there's a twelve-hour "window" during those days when the mating will occur. Otherwise, the female won't tolerate the male's advances. Estrus occurs during the night, which is the normal activity time for hamsters.

All you have to do is to introduce the female into the male's cage every evening for four days. You can tell if she'll probably be receptive by stroking her back. If she flattens her body, and splays her legs out, she should be receptive to the male—unless she doesn't seem to find that male attractive; female hamsters don't always behave as we predict they should. When you place the female into the male's cage, there may be some initial sparring, but only minor tussles. If breeding is going to take place, it will happen in the first half hour (or far less) that they are together.

If she's interested, female hamsters leave little to chance when they are ready to mate. A receptive female uses lordosis to indicate her readiness to breed; she runs over to the male, and does sort of a pushup, as she did when you stroked her back, with her legs splayed and the forearms straight. If the female signals her readiness, the male will sniff her head, her ears (remember those scent glands), and her genital area. He will mount her from behind, breed, and dismount. He repeats this action several times in just a few minutes.

Be ready to remove the female if she wants only to fight with the male; wear gloves or back one of the hamsters into a can or jar so you won't get bitten. It also helps if the male has some easy-to-get-to hiding places, so he can discreetly duck out if the female gets mean.

If mating occurs, keep the pair together for a few hours or even overnight, the big exception being the Chinese hamsters. With Chinese

When in estrus, the receptive breeding stage, the female will assume the lordosis position when a male hamster is present.

Female winter whites can block a pregnancy if the male is removed from the cage.

hamsters, the female is so aggressive, you'll need to remove her after two hours; this is one of the reasons it took us so long to figure out how to breed this species in captivity. When you separate the Chinese hamsters, the male should still be in his own cage. Do not try to tidy things up by placing him in with other males; the other males will probably attack him (of course they know what's going on, because of their ability to interpret scents).

Campbell's pairs can be left together. Winter white pairs must be left together or the female will block the egg implantation (see page 23 for more on this ability).

Did the Mating "Take?"

Whether you keep your Campbell's/winter whites in colonies, or you keep individual Roborovski, Chinese, or Syrians, if there's any chance mating may have occurred,

look at the females each morning. The morning after mating, the female may have a copulatory plug, a waxy whitish plug in the opening of the vagina. This is an indication that sperm were released during the mating. Females also have a whitish vaginal discharge for about five days after mating. You can also expect that a pregnant female will be hostile to a male, when she is placed in his cage.

When Sexual Maturity Occurs

How quickly female hamsters come into estrus depends to some degree on the type of hamster, and how they are housed. Campbell's hamsters, little social busybodies that they are, are a good example. When female Campbell's are housed with unfamiliar males at weaning, they begin their estrous cycle earlier than Campbell's housed singly or with their siblings and parents. If Campbell's are kept only with sibling females, the females not only grow more slowly and weigh less, but their estrus is delayed—after all, why rush since nothing can happen anyway. Mature females housed with familiar males conceive much slower than mature females housed with unfamiliar males.

But the unsocial Syrians don't behave like the Campbell's. No matter if they are housed with adult males, sibling females, or alone, there is no change in their maturation rates. At about 45 days old, they're out of the nest, have found a nest site, and are ready for a mate.

The Estrous Cycle

Hamsters are sexually mature at six to seven weeks of age. During the breeding season of late spring through early fall, hamsters come into season every four days, if food supplies are adequate. In the wild, the estrous cycle is naturally altered by day length and food intake. Short days mean winter, which means restricted food, and the females won't come into their cycle. This is a survival response that keeps the female from becoming pregnant and bearing young, both requiring high-energy output, as any mother will tell you, when she'll have trouble finding food for herself, and her young would have trouble finding food once weaned. Under artificial lighting, hamsters may stay on their long-day cycle, which means

pregnancy can occur in the dead of winter.

The short estrous cycle helps explain why a female can get pregnant so quickly. She'll be interested, on the average, one day in four, although she'll solicit a male the day before her receptive day. Females signal sexual receptivity by secretion of pheromones (hormonal scents) and the lordosis pose; there may be ultrasonic vocalizations as well.

Adult Syrians are reproductively active and at their lowest weight (fighting trim, as it was once called) during the long days, or during the summer. Once winter sets in—the short days—the food resources become limited, the reproductive urge switches off, and bulking up to survive the winter months becomes the priority.

Gestation

A number of behavioral changes occur in the pregnant hamster. They get fatter, especially 10 to 18 days after the mating. For Syrian hamsters, the female, not surprisingly,

Female Syrians come into their first estrus at 45 days.

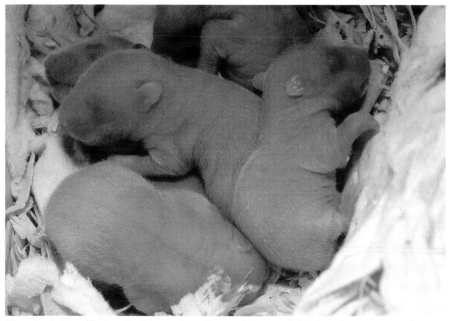

Hamster babies (Syrians in this case) are born hairless and sightless, but not squeak-less!

spends less time wheel running and more time eating and in the nest area. Females kept in ground-level burrows spend more time digging, while those in wire cages show more gnawing behavior at the beginning of the pregnancy. The researcher M. Daly suggested that in nature, early pregnancy signals the time for more elaborate burrow construction for litter-related activities. Pregnant hamsters tend to become very aggressive as their due date nears. If you're been pregnant yourself, you probably understand.

Pregnant Syrians often display the receptive-to-mating pose near the end of the pregnancy period, although the pose is displayed for only a short period of time. The aggression normally displayed by the females is enhanced during pregnancy, and even more so during lactation, but this may be a well-instilled reaction to perceived threats to the young.

The Birth

How can you tell if your female is about to give birth? Watch the female in question. Female Syrians increase their respiration rate by 50 percent when they are due to give birth within the next several hours. The nest-building activity goes into high gear, along with eating, grooming, and digging. The female will seem restless and may startle easily; the researcher, T. E. Rowell said the sudden movement looked like "a drowsing person bitten by an insect." The female stands erect. As the pups are born, she severs the umbilical cord. Syrians may eat the placenta; Campbell's or winter whites may add the placenta to the food store.

The mother holds her new babies and cleans them. Pups are born at 10- to 30-minute intervals, and the female sleeps or tidies the nest area between births. The birth process generally takes about two hours, and by that time the mother has gathered all the young around her and curls her body over them. Expect her to be very hungry and very thirsty; she has to eat and drink for five (or eight... or fifteen). Your role is to bring food and water, and to make sure the young pups can reach the nozzle of the water bottle when they begin to wander out of the nest. Keep your nose out of the cage.

Although your hamster may give birth to 5 to 15 babies, she may not raise all of them to weaning. She may eat them instead.

Ick! My Hamster Ate Her Babies!

We don't know if hamsters in the wild cannibalize their young, other than the lamentable example set by that first wild-caught mother hamster back in 1930, but this activity is certainly common in laboratory and pet hamsters.

What we do know is that cannibalism is not at all limited to new mothers. Sometimes there are clues

Syrian hamster females are particularly sensitive about nest box intrusions until the young are two weeks old.

that the mother-pup relationship isn't a strong one. A surprising number of laboratory births—some 25 percent of those *observed*—are abnormal, in that the mother seemed to be unable to bond with the young. The mother may seem jumpy, as if she can't stand to have the babies nurse from her, jerking away when they contact her. Those females actually leave the nest when

Campbell's hamsters have litters of four to six pups, and the female can become pregnant within a month.

Even babies as old as ten days may be destroyed if the mother feels threatened.

the young try to nurse from her, and then will return to the nest to kill and eat some or all of the litter.

The second type of abnormal birth is when the young are born outside of the nest area, these pups are likely to be ignored or cannibalized. So if your female hamster seems jumpy, or births her young outside of the nest area, expect the worst.

Admittedly, new mothers can be extremely touchy about their young. When new mothers have their babies taken away from them, and are presented with young of the same age that are not theirs, they kill the pups. In contrast, female hamsters that have had pups in the past generally feed the unrelated young.

Pup destruction is not limited to the first few days of birth, although the incidence of cannibalism is highest for the first two days after parturition. The mother may kill all or part of the litter (this latter is more common) any time from parturition to 14 days after the birth.

Researchers have tried to find the key to pup destruction. It isn't related to the age of the mother when she was mated, or litter size, or the appearance of the pups, the amount of food hoarded, or if the female cannibalized earlier litters.

We have found that the incidence of pup destruction is highest during the first few days after parturition. Mother hamsters were given foster pups the same day as giving birth, either in addition to their young or as substitutes for pups that were removed. The females demonstrated cannibalism that was proportional (not equal) to the number of pups added or removed. Control mothers, who had no changes to their litters, killed about two pups. Mothers given two to four pups killed an average of four and six pups. Mothers given six pups cannibalized almost seven pups. Day and Galef concluded that cannibalism was related to the mother's effort to regulate the number of pups in relation to environmental demands, although all the hamsters in the study had unlimited access to food and water. I see it as a control issue; the more change in the pup situation—the more the nest site is invaded—the less the mother wants to do with the pups.

When you suspect there are young in the nest, simply do nothing. When your female hamster gets fat and then you don't see her for a day or two, leave her alone. I think it's probably better if she has a dark, enclosed area—a burrow, if you will—to give birth in. Mother hamsters need serious privacy for a week after giving birth. If you open the cage to look at the young, don't be surprised if your female interprets this gesture as a threat and eats her young. Hamsters have small brains and they don't work very hard at trying to figure the reason behind one of your actions. If she has babies and the birthing site isn't secure, a female will eat her young because there's no other "safe" place for them. (You may think a cage is roomy, but it isn't all that big.)

You'll find out soon enough if there are babies within the cage. After a few days, if you pause near the cage, you'll hear the young squeaking. Evidently there's a lot to talk about when you have to share your mother's teats (depending on the type, from three to six pairs will be available) with a bunch of hungry siblings, and keep in mind all you're hearing are the sonic vocalizations. The ultrasonics are, in a manner of speaking, way over your head.

The stress leading to cannibalism may be internal, such as poor health. There are other stressors that can cause cannibalism. Cold is one. Mother Syrians maintained at 50°F (10°C) eat more of their babies than those maintained at 72°F (22°C). Not enough food is another—but of course a conscientious pet owner will make sure there's plenty to eat in the cage.

Hamster Development

One day you awaken, stretch, and get out of bed to check on your hamsters. You have a pair of Syrians that of course are kept in separate cages, but you're pretty certain the female is pregnant. She's been eating like a horse, and she's distinctly rounded across the lower half of her body when she stands upright to take a treat.

As you pad over to the cage of the female, you hear squeaking, little tiny squeaks, not adult-sized. The female is hidden in her bedding and she doesn't respond when you tell her it's time to brush her teeth. (She doesn't really brush her teeth; she just crawls into your cupped hands from her opened door and then explores your bathroom while you brush your teeth, a daily ritual you both rather enjoy.)

Baby Roborovski show their coat patterns early.

Gestation, Litter Size, and Weaning Ages

Breed	Gestation	Litter Size	Weaning Age
Syrian	15–18 days	4–12	21 days
Campbell's	18–22 days	8	21 days
Winter Whites	18–22 days	4–6	20 days
Roborovski	20–22 days	3–5	19 days
Chinese	20–21 days	4–5	21 days

Looks like—nope, make that *sounds* like, you have babies. No, you can't check any further, not for at least a week, and you're on your own as far as brushing your teeth for at least three weeks. Here's what's happening behind those closed (cage) doors:

Day One

They can't see, but they can squeak, and they communicate with their mother (and any other hamster that's within hearing distance) about being hungry, being jostled, and what-ever else can pass through the mind of a very young hamster. They drink milk from their mother, often sharing teats with their siblings. You should not bother them, but these are little red embryo-looking babies that eat so enthusiastically that the milk they drink can be seen through the thin skin over their stomach. They have tiny teeth, to grip the mother's teat.

Two to Three Days

Some pigment begins to develop in the skin, but only for those babies

Ten-day old Campbell's display coat patterns.

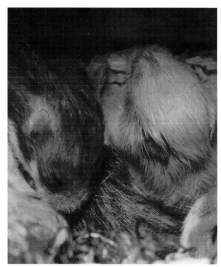

Syrian pups at about 10 days, eyes still closed.

Even with closed eyes, pups need and seek out sources of moisture.

Five-day old Campbell's.

that will have dark skin or dark patches of skin. You won't be able to see what color they'll develop yet, and don't even think about peeking—these babies are too young!

Four to Five Days

The little ear canals under the little rosy waxy-looking ears have opened, and the babies can hear much better (when you're this young, you can feel your mother's heartbeat more than you can hear it). A faint sheen of fur begins to appear.

Six to Ten Days

The ears bear a short patina of fur. The body has short fur all over it, and at ten days the babies are rolling out of the nest site and beginning to nibble on solid food, even if their eyes aren't open. You can see a line where the eyelids will open, if you sneak a peak while the young are staggering around in the cage.

Ten to Fifteen Days

The fur colors are identifiable (mostly), and the eyes begin to open; the eyes will fully open by 14–16 days. You can see the flank glands on the Syrians. The ventral gland on the belly of the dwarfs becomes noticeable. Babies are

Young Syrians at 16 days still huddle, but this habit will disappear.

Ways to Find Homes for Your Young Hamsters

• Place ads in the "Pets" section of the classifieds in your local newspapers. Although your big daily paper may reach more people, the classified ads in smaller weeklies tend to have a higher readership.

• Thumbtack 3 × 5 cards on feed store and business bulletin boards. Be sure you add a date on the card, so whoever decides to clean up the bulletin board will have some idea of how long your card has been in place. Start with an appealing headline such as "Small Bodies, Big Hearts, Likes Children." If you put the asking price on the card, everyone knows the hamsters are for sale. If you're giving them away, you may not want to say right out that they are free; you may want to sound out any callers before you get around to the price. People do feed hamsters to snakes, and if this bothers you, you have the right not to let just anyone have your babies.

• Contact your local home-schooling alliance. Parents who home-school their children are eager for their children to learn responsibility, and enjoy rewarding their children for good behavior.

• Contact the elementary teachers and the high school science teachers in your public schools through the principals and the sciences coordinators. All teachers want their students to learn responsibility and to enjoy learning.

• If you have your own web page, keyword "hamsters" and your page will appear when people do a search. You'll have to put your state in your ad, so a surfer in Oregon can skip over a hamster ad from Virginia.

• Tell your friends that you have hamsters for sale, and ask them to let any of their friends know. This technique is most effective if children are involved.

---

more comfortable wandering from the nest, and the mother doesn't haul them back quite so quickly. In the wild, the babies would just wander about the nest and food larders, so they'd be safe there as well. Babies begin to drink from the drinking tube and to nibble on bits of fresh apple, as an additional water source. They may try drinking water at 13–15 days.

Sixteen to Twenty-one Days

The hamsters have essentially fully erupted teeth, and they can eat with enthusiasm—and they do. Because they can chow down solid food, their growth rate accelerates. By the end of three weeks, they are tiny versions of the parents, and if you could sell them at this tender age, they'd be snapped up like peanuts. With a body length of 1 inch to 2½ inches (2.5–6.4 cm), the young are irresistible. They all need access to fresh water by this age, so make certain the tube is set low enough. They like carrots and apples, too. If you have a litter of both the dwarf types and the Syrians, you'll see that both types play with their siblings, but the play modes are a bit different. The Syrians may be less likely to cuddle up after playing than the dwarf species.

Twenty-one to Twenty-eight Days

Instead of little tiny hamsters, you've got a cage full of young adults, better developed and just a bit thicker through the body than those of just a week ago. The young are fully weaned, and the mother is capable of breeding again!

Twenty-eight to Thirty-five Days

The young adult hamsters are now sexually mature. If you're in a short-day cycle, the males will mate with any receptive females, and they don't recognize any societal barriers to mating. Yes, of course a son will breed with his mother or his sisters; that's how breeders develop some of those beautiful colors. If you aren't ready to become a breeder and to face the challenge of finding good homes for up to a dozen hamsters from the *next* litter, separate the males from the females. If these are the dwarf hamsters, the females can live together in one group and the males in another group; if they're together as siblings,

At one year, this blue fawn Campbell's has reached middle age.

males only rarely fight with each other. If these are Syrians, find a way to cage each individually.

Thirty-five Days to Three Months

This is the ideal period to sell your baby hamsters. They're fully weaned, perfectly independent (but try to sell same-sex pairs of the Campbell's, because they are quite social little rodents), and very appealing in their just less than adult sizing.

Twelve to Fourteen Months

The hamsters begin to approach middle age. The female Syrians, Campbell's, and winter whites are less fertile, although the males of each species are still very potent.

Fourteen to Sixteen Months

The hamsters begin to show their age. The fur thins, especially on the ears. The hamster looks just a bit

If a Syrian hamster is mated in the afternoon just before estrus starts, or on the morning of estrus, she'll have a larger litter and more females than males than matings that occur later in estrus. So if you're breeding your Syrian, and you want a higher percentage of males than females in the litter, mate the female toward the end of the fertility cycle.

scruffy and unkempt. The hamster sleeps more and eats slightly less. The females are infertile.

Eighteen to Forty-eight Months

Activity decreases and hamsters find sleep more appealing than wandering around the cage. The males (at last!) become sterile. Hamster movements are slow and more cautious.

Although Syrian young have a shorter gestation than the other hamster breeds, they develop faster in utero.

The Maternal Instinct

Hamsters and other rodents have been so well studied and analyzed that researchers can point to hormone level changes in a blood profile and say, "It's at this point, with the estrogen levels rising, that the female becomes maternal and will choose to feed and care for her newly born pups."

The ironic part is that these hormone levels don't stay high. There's a mystery at work here, because the mother hamster feeds and tidies up her young, but the hormone levels that first precipitated this behavior decline. When the young are most dependent on the mother's care, and the estrogen levels are high, she spends her time licking them, constructing/fluffing up the nest, nursing, and hauling back the tiny pups that decide to check out the world outside the nest. "You there, pup number 10, get back in here, on the double!" and then sighing "Oh, well" and bounding out of the nest, babies still nursing, grabbing the adventurous pup by its head and hauling it back into the nest. (As a matter of interest and as a plea for more natural nesting sites, those pups raised in a modified burrow setup as opposed to a wire cage tended to wander away from the nest less than those in a wire cage.) As the pups get older and need a bit less of this almost-fussy tending, the activity displayed by the female parent declines, along with her estrogen levels. If you fool her by replacing her maturing pups with younger pups that still need the massive amounts of tending, her parental behavior will be prolonged.

As the young become more independent, the mother's involvement with her young decreases. For brief periods, she moves about the cage and climbs onto objects, sniffs the environs, grooms herself, rears up on her hind legs—almost as if she didn't have a half-dozen or more hungry mouths back in the nest. For first-time mothers, this urge to get out and look around shows a marked increase 15 days after the birth of her young, and for mothers of multiple litters, it occurs on day 18. If the pups are removed for a short time and then put back in the nest, as the estrogen level begins to decline, the mother exhibits "deficiencies in maternal responsiveness."

Syrians have a short gestation period of just 16 days. The Campbell's (or Winter Whites), have a gestation of 18 days, and the Chinese, 20 days. Of those three, the Syrians develop more rapidly during gestation than the other two species, so all young are born at about the same state of development. The different species move through the development stages (first grooming signs, independent defecation) at differing rates.

Pup Development

Hamsters are groomers. Syrian hamsters begin grooming themselves by the second week of life, moving their forepaws over the snout without touching it. By the second week, they begin licking their forepaws and brushing about the head and the snout. At 15 days they begin coordinated licking and brushing of the entire body. No matter what the species of hamster, the head and snout grooming appears about the same time the young begin nibbling at solid food, and the whole body brushing occurs when the young take forays out of the nest area and begin to eliminate urine and feces without the mother's stimulation. (All these figures are from hamsters observed in captivity; none are from hamsters in the wild.)

Pups huddle with each other, move around with each other, and eat together. They also begin play-fighting. Huddling is especially important while the pups are young, so everyone stays warm as very young mammals aren't very good at moderating their body temperature. When the dam or female leaves the nest in the fourth or fifth week postpartum, the pups themselves begin to seek their own independent nest sites. The mother may move to another corner of the cage for her new nest, and again to another site. The abandoned nests are effectively dismantled by the pups as they enter and leave the nest, and steal portions of it for their own nests.

Once the pups are weaned (at about 25 days), and before they reach puberty (at 45 days), they spend the first ten days ending their relationship with their mother and establishing their own nests.

Chapter Eight

Hamster Health

Hamsters are subject to few health problems and very few diseases, which is one of the many reasons they make such good pets. They are easy to keep healthy because prevention (or to use a modern term, "wellness") isn't difficult and it isn't expensive.

All hamsters need ready access to fresh water.

Disease Prevention

Prevention heads off problems before they can start.

Diet: Good diet is one means of prevention (see Diet, Chapter Five). A good diet prevents weakened bones and a variety of vitamin-deficiency diseases. A good commercial hamster food is your best defense against illness of any sort, but not all commercial hamster foods are created equal. Hamster breeders are vociferous about the pros and cons of different brands of hamster diets. If you keep a hamster colony and your hamsters are ill and dying at a young age without any obvious pathogens or genetic problems, consider changing the food you offer. If a different brand of hamster food would help or end whatever problem your hamsters are having, it's an inexpensive solution.

Water: Your hamster always needs a ready supply of clean drinking water, especially if it is a nursing mother. Her young need water, too; this is particularly true of winter whites. Babies may be stunted if they don't have access to the drinking tube or to chewable water sources such as fresh apple or cucumber pieces.

Avoiding drafts: Is your hamster cage located in a draft-free area? Hamsters dig burrows to protect themselves from unfavorable conditions; they can't do that very well in your caging. If you live in a northern climate and keep your hamsters in a room that gets drafty in the winter, use a cage that will forestall drafts; in a case like this, an aquarium would be a good choice for a hamster cage. Just make sure it's large enough.

Avoiding dampness: Is the hamster being kept in an area that's too damp? Hamsters evolved in deserts and grassy plains, and they are adapted to lower humidity levels. The Campbell's hamster excretes concentrated urine to conserve moisture. Don't keep your pet in a damp, enclosed area; move the cage to a drier part of the house.

Hiding places: Hamsters, even those social species, need hiding places. This gives each individual hamster a way to avoid the stress of group living in a cage. Put a few sleeping boxes or the cores from paper towels in the cage, to offer privacy to those that might need it. A few pieces of paper toweling or toilet paper squares will give them the distraction of fluffing up the bedding. If your winter whites are like mine, they'll provide you some distraction by urinating on their bedding, so you can change it every few days or so.

A healthy hamster is an active, happy explorer.

Exercise: You already know about the benefits of exercise for humans, hamsters are no exception. An exercise wheel gives them a chance to exercise regularly and to relieve stress. If the cage is too small for an exercise wheel, get a bigger cage; experiments have shown that hamsters that are moved from small cages to larger cages spend less time in their exercise wheel (but they still use it).

Avoiding falls: Avoid falls always. When you handle your hamster, hang onto it so it can't wiggle out of your hands and dive like a fur-covered sausage to the floor below. (Holding your hamster in any of the three hamster holds (see page 77) also prevents damage to you when your hamster tries to turn around and give you a good nip.)

Even young Syrians seek out water sources.

Safe toys: Providing only safe chew toys will avoid stomach blockage when your hamster manages to nibble its way through part of the chew toy.

Avoiding bites: Bites from other cagemates can fail to heal and cause abscesses. Caging Syrian or unacquainted dwarf hamsters separately will avoid fighting and damage from bites.

Detecting Illness

You and your hamster may enjoy every moment of its life together with nary even a sniffle on either part. But this dispassionate attitude will fly out the window the day you look in your hamster's cage and it is crouched in a corner with fur ruffed up and once bright eyes looking dull. Hamsters are so small that their body reserves are used up quickly.

Your sick hamster needs help or it may die.

• Are there any other signs of hamster illness? Watch your hamster; its behavior will tell you. Look at it when it wakes up. Hamsters tend to go through a specific set of behaviors when they awaken, much as humans do—they awaken, stretch, and yawn with the mouth wide open. Then they do a quick grooming, rather a combined scratching and straightening of the fur.

• What is the reaction when you open the cage door? Hamsters that feel good tend to regard the opening of the cage door as a good sign, possibly meaning food. Their noses go up in the air and you can see their whiskers vibrating and the upper lip lifted as they pick up and try to interpret the signs. Worth getting out of bed for? Is it possibly a live grasshopper? Or gee, it's only that person again, I'm going back to sleep.

• If your hamster has a satin coat, is the fur smooth and sleek? Healthy hamsters have a sleek coat. If you have a rex, when they're ill, their coat seems ruffled and dry looking.

• Do your hamster's eyes look bright and alert? A healthy hamster has shiny eyes and there's no discharge in the corners of the eyes.

• Look at your hamster's nose. The nose should be dry but not runny.

• Finally, lift your hamster up and check the anal area. Is it dry? A wet anal area, or a hamster sitting in his own feces and not moving to a dry spot in the cage is a bad sign.

Rate Yourself on Prevention

Give yourself five points for every question you can answer "Yes."

	Yes	No
Is my hamster's diet the best I can find and is the protein content about 15 percent or higher?	___	___
Is the food fresh?	___	___
Is the drinking water always clean and can everyone in the cage reach the drinking tube?	___	___
Do I clean the cage every week, and change the bedding as well?	___	___
Is the caging located in an area that isn't too damp, and is the hamster cage located where the hamster has a chance to look out at the world around him?	___	___
Do I hold my hamster enough so it isn't frightened of me, and do I give it a brief health inspection every week or so?	___	___
Do I provide chew toys and an exercise wheel for my hamster?	___	___

Evaluation:
30–35 points—You know what you're doing.
20–25 points—You need to work harder at hamster caretaking.
Under 20 points—What are you doing? Are you sure you want a hamster?

A quick stretch and grooming are signs of health.

Full cheek pouches mean a trip to the bedroom food stash.

• Hamsters that don't feel good tend to tune out the world. Hamsters that are ill generally don't drink water, and they won't eat. They have a "leave me alone" distracted attitude and act briefly nippy if you bother them. They sit hunched over, as if to protect their body. The eyes are dull, teary, and may look sunken, partly due to the disease process and partly due to loss of body moisture or dehydration. You need to do something.

First Actions

What do you do until you figure out what is wrong and either fix it yourself or take your pet to your veterinarian? First of all, if your hamster isn't alone, separate it from all other hamsters, and all animals, for that matter. Put the cage in an area or niche that's in the 70–85°F (21–29°C)

This Syrian is alert, probably hoping for a treat.

temperature range. If your hamster is in a wire mesh or wire-barred cage, make sure that the room is free from drafts, or that you cover one end of the cage to provide a draft-free area. It might even be best if the cage is in a room other than the usual hamster room, if only to remind you when you see the cage that the hamster within needs special tending.

If your hamster has diarrhea and the cage is dirty as a result, clean the cage, but disturb your pet as little as possible while you do this. Wash your hands before you start. If the hamster is in a sleeping box, you can lift out the sleeping box with the hamster inside, put in fresh substrate and bedding, and put the box back in the cage. Be especially careful when you come into contact with a sick hamster's feces. Dried aerosol from feces can literally drift anywhere and be inhaled by you or any other breathing creature—not a good idea when your hamster is sick.

If there are any toys or an exercise wheel in the cages, wash them in soapy water, then dunk them in a solution of 10 percent bleach (this is 10 percent by volume, or ¼ cup of bleach to 2¼ cups of water). Then rinse well, so there is no detectable odor of bleach (if you can smell it with that great huge insensitive nose of yours, think of what it must smell like to your sick hammie), let them dry, and put them back in the cage. Take the discarded substrate and bedding material out to your garbage can.

Replace the food and water. Wash your hands again, so you won't

Signs of Illness in Hamsters

- Little or no interest in food
- Loss of weight
- Change in awake/sleep cycle
- Eyes: reddening of the conjunctiva, discharge, adhered eyelids
- Behavior changes: increased aggression, depression, reluctance to move around
- Posture: curled position although hamster is awake, rigid standing, stiff gait
- Appearance: wet tail, diarrhea, loss of hair, scaly skin

spread any possible "bug" to other hamsters, other pets, your family, or to yourself.

Talk to Your Veterinarian

Call your veterinarian and tell him or her about the symptoms you've noticed, and how long your hamster has been ill.

Ask about the fees, if you're concerned about the potential costs. If you're a new client of the veterinarian, you'll feel better if you know something about fees for hamster care. Most veterinarians are very reasonable about charging for pocket pets.

Sometimes the problem is so minute that your veterinarian can offer a suggestion over the phone, if he or she has already seen your hamster. But if your veterinarian hasn't seen your hamster before, or if your hamster isn't eating or drinking, you'll need to take your hamster

in to be seen. If your hammie is sick, and your veterinarian has evening hours, make an appointment in the evening so your hamster will be naturally awake. Transport your hamster in its cage, if it's a transportable cage. Since my hamsters were in a rack system with kitty litter trays, I used a deep plastic bucket with fresh shavings on the bottom. Since the bucket was about 18 inches (76 cm) deep, I wasn't worried about drafts. If you're going out in cold weather, you might want to cover the bucket or cage with a towel.

Your veterinarian will probably ask you some questions about your hamster. He or she may not know that there are five kinds available, so be prepared to discuss a little about your hamster: what species it is, how old it is, what you feed it, how long you've had it, whether there are any new hamsters in your house, and how long your hamster has been sick. He or she may ask if there have been any changes in your

A sick hamster shuts out the world. Its coat is roughened, and its eyes are dull.

115

Antibiotics That Will Kill Your Hamster

Hamsters can tolerate many antibiotics, but a few of them will kill good bacteria and let the wrong kind of bacteria grow, or bloom. One of these pathogens is the botulism bacteria, *Clostridium difficile*. Botulism bacteria won't directly kill your hamster, but they excrete a toxin that is deadly to hamsters as well as to humans. So make a copy of this antibiotic list and don't forget it when you visit your veterinarian with your hamster, should your hamster become ill. Your veterinarian is extremely knowledgeable but there's a lot to remember when you're treating different kinds of animals. You are also extremely bright and would never, *ever,* dose your hamsters with your own leftover antibiotics.

Do Not Use
- Penicillin
- Ampicillin
- Erythromycin
- Lincomycin
- Vancomycin
- The cephalosporins

Using these will cause death, preceded by loss of appetite (anoxia) and diarrhea.

household, such as a newly installed air conditioner, or if any chemicals have been in use around the house (painting your house qualifies as chemical use in this case). Offer to take your hamster out of the cage and hand it to your veterinarian. Many animals are territorial about their cages, and veterinarians try to avoid getting bitten.

Hamster Ailments

Hamster diseases are generally grouped by the causative agent. We'll begin with what I'll call mechanical problems, which are pretty straightforward and easy to correct. The actual healing may take some time, but at least the cause is easy to identify and correct.

Broken Bones

Your hamster takes a flying leap off a tabletop and lands heavily. When you pick her up, you notice she won't put any weight on her fore limb, and she seems to be in pain. She may have broken a leg. Put her in her own cage, away from everything else. Take out the wheel and any toys. If you think the leg is broken, you can call your veterinarian for assistance, but hamsters are too small to splint or cast, and they'll just chew off any sort of bandage when you're not looking. Watch your hamster carefully for 12 to 24 hours to make sure that there's nothing wrong other than the leg. To be blunt, if there's internal bleeding, your hamster will die within 6 to 12 hours. There's nothing you can do for internal bleeding; there's no sort of animal trauma surgery show on TV to spur veterinarians into funding and building trauma centers for animals, and few people want to spend $1,000 or so on emergency abdominal surgery for their hamster. Hamster breeders I've talked to on this "what if" scenario assure me that broken limbs heal quite nicely within two weeks if the hamster is isolated, placed in a cage without a wheel, not handled, and fed a good diet with a calcium supplement.

Bites

Hamsters do tend to fight with each other, and bites are part of that scenario. It doesn't seem to matter who starts a fight, or even what sex the combatants are. Because caging isn't big enough for hamsters to escape each other, fighting and the stress of being on guard tends to go on and on, with only short breaks in between. Unless you're right on hand and intervene, there's a winner and a loser.

To inspect your hamster for bite marks, hold it in your hands and run your fingertips gently over its body. You're going to feel for rough spots on the skin, which can be healed bite marks, for swellings, and for tender spots, which can be unhealed wounds. The vast majority of times, bites heal well without any intervention on your part, but if you find an open wound, clean it with hydrogen peroxide or soap and water. If you use soap and water, be certain to rinse the wound well. Remember that hamsters are groomers, and they'll lick off anything you put on their fur.

Any change in normal behavior may be an indication of illness.

Abscesses

Sometimes a wound heals over before the infection inside is eliminated. Damaged tissue and bacteria are sealed inside and the infection continues to exist. The result is a sealed-off infection (an abscess), a pocket containing damaged tissue and pus (a combination of bacteria and the carcasses of white blood cells that have swallowed up bacteria and died as a result). Abscesses aren't contagious in the usual sense, although the bacteria they contain can certainly cause abscesses in other hamsters if those hamsters have wounds.

Abscesses look like swollen areas on the hamsters' body or on its limbs. These areas are also very tender to the touch, partially because of the pressure they exert on neighboring healthy tissue, the destruction of the tissue within them, and because of

Has your hamster become reclusive? Check with your ears first—are there babies in that house?

the toxins secreted by the bacterial contents. Some abscesses are actually hard to the touch, which tells you something of the pressure within. Other symptoms include redness of the skin over and surrounding the abscess (you can simply blow the fur

The satin coat on a Rob looks greasy— this is just the way the coat looks.

aside to see the color of the skin— even the lightest touch of your hand will be painful). Your hamster may clearly display concern about the site, scratching it or around it, or endlessly grooming the fur around the site. If the abscess is on the face, expect to see drooling, facial swelling, perhaps bad breath (you'd have to get close to experience this). Lack of appetite, depression/lack of activity, and weight loss are other typical symptoms, and learning of the discomfort abscesses can cause, you can certainly understand *why*.

Your veterinarian will use a syringe and the fine needle to try to aspirate some of the pus from within the abscess. Don't be surprised if some of the pus dribbles out of the puncture wound made by the needle, but most of the contents are too thick to go through a needle. Ultrasound or radiograph may be used to determine the size of the abscess.

Syrian babies huddle and get along, but fights will erupt when they get to be just over a month old.

Depending on the site and the size of the abscess, your veterinarian may drain it after using a sterile scalpel to create a tiny nick into the abscess. Further treatment may be needed, or at least an anesthetic administered to put your hamster to sleep while the area is opened and cleaned. Hamsters can die of shock when "wounded" by humans without an anesthetic. Hamsters can deal with wounds inflicted by other hamsters far more calmly than wounds inflicted by "barbaric" humans.

After the abscess has been opened and cleaned, an antibiotic powder or liquid is usually sprinkled around or injected into the former abscess site, and then administered, probably orally, for a few days afterward, to ensure that the bacteria are eliminated.

Once the abscess has been treated, your hamster should regain its appetite and any weight loss.

Eyes

Hamsters do develop eye problems in response to eye injuries or infections. Some kinds of Campbell's hamsters are born without eyes. Hamsters also develop cataracts. If your hamster keeps its eye closed, as if they hurt, put the cage in a darkened area. You might

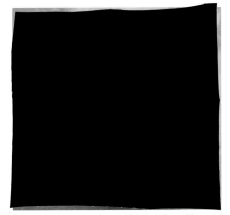

Hamster's eyes should be bright with no discharge, but they can be damaged by injury or infection.

119

My Hamster Died and I Don't Know Why

In a worst-case scenario, if your hamster has died and you really, *really* want to find out what happened, yes, you can have a necropsy performed. There are commercial necropsy labs, but most of them aren't set up to work on animal tissues. Veterinary colleges are your best bet in locating an animal research lab that will perform necropsies for a fee. But be forewarned: Necropsies aren't cheap, and you must provide what are called fixed specimens so the necropsy can be made.

When your hamster dies, tissue samples must be fixed before anything changes in the body. Once the animal is dead, whatever bacteria the immune system had been keeping at bay, and those the immune system could not stop, are unimpeded, and they'll grow rampantly. In less than 12 hours, what-

Call your veterinarian, and ask him or her to fix tissue specimens for the necropsy. Put your hamster's body in a cooler, add some ice, and take the cooler to your veterinarian. He or she will take a stool specimen, lung, heart, brains, liver, spleen, and other tissue samples, and immerse them in small bottles of formalin solution. Either you or your veterinarian need to call the necropsy lab, to find out exactly which samples to take and to check on shipping regulations (shipping regulations can change rapidly, so you'll need up-to-date information) and on shipping containers. Your veterinarian will probably do the packing and shipping for you, just as a matter of procedure and to avoid the possibility of anything going wrong with the tissue samples. You'll need to ship the container via an overnight express service, but the necropsy company will give you details.

Cheek Pouch Injury

Your hamster's cheek pouches may be bitten in a fight, or your hamster may find a sharp object in the cage and damage its cheek pouches. If your hamster seems unable to empty the cheek pouches, hold it on its back with the nape hold and try to see what the problem is. You may need to get your veterinarian's help to remove foreign objects from your hamster's cheek pouches, but don't delay. Cheek pouches are used in research for skin grafts because the pouches are not immunologically active; grafts in the cheek pouches are rejected less than grafts in any other part of the body. This means that the pouches are less capable of fighting off an injury or infection. In addition, a hamster with cheek pouch problems is in all likelihood not eating.

Teeth

Hamsters' front incisors are designed to rub against each other when they're nibbling on something, and they are supposed to wear evenly. This doesn't always happen. Hamsters need their front teeth to be perfectly aligned so they can eat. When the teeth don't wear evenly, the unmatched teeth may grow into the roof of the mouth or into the pouches. This may be a genetic problem and you don't need to breed this hamster, but in the meantime, you need to help your hamster. There are no nerve endings in the teeth, just in the very base of each tooth, and in the roots.

To check your hamster's teeth, put your hamster in a nape hold and look at the teeth. If you see that one tooth is longer than its mate, you can use a pair of fingernail clippers to gently trim the offending tooth. Nip off tiny bits at a time until the teeth are aligned. If this is more than you want to take on, your veterinarian can trim your hamster's teeth.

Check the teeth once a month so you can get the problem corrected if it reoccurs.

If the tooth base seems inflamed or the face or gums swollen, take

The famous nape hold is a good way to immobilize your hamster so you can inspect its teeth and cheek pouches.

your hamster to your veterinarian who may extract the infected tooth and prescribe antibiotics until the gum heals.

Cheek teeth: Sometimes the cheek teeth are the site of the problem. Unlike rabbits, whose continuously growing cheek teeth may be prone to periodontal disease and abscesses, the hamsters (and mice, rats, and gerbils) have short-crowned, rooted cheek teeth that are subject to cavities and periodontal disease. Try to avoid sugar-laden treats and snacks. Your veterinarian can help by tooth extraction and antibiotics, but this is a largely avoidable problem and an expense few owners are willing to incur.

Ears

Hamsters do develop ear problems. Symptoms are holding the head tilted to one side, shaking the head, and scratching the ear area with the foot. You won't be able to

Hamsters are desert creatures, but they are as subject to heatstroke as any mammal.

see inside your hamster's ear without an otoscope, so you'll need to see your veterinarian for assistance on a possible ear problem. If you want to ease the itching overnight, add a drop of mineral oil to a cotton swab and gently clean/wipe the hamster's ears. If the itching doesn't stop, see your veterinarian.

Heatstroke

Although hamsters are desert animals, they burrow to avoid the heat. Some burrows are 8 feet (2.4 m) deep, so for hamsters in the desert, heat isn't a problem. When your hamster's cage is near a sunny window, in your car, or in an unventilated room, it can't avoid the heat. Your hamster may cope by breathing heavily, and lying on its belly to expose more of the body for cooling off. It may become semiconscious. Your hamster will die very quickly, and in distress, unless you take steps immediately. Move the cage to

a cool spot, take the hamster out, and run cool (not cold) water over its body until it is alert and the high breathing rate has slowed. Dry it off gently, and put it in a clean, dry cage away from any heat to rest. The cage should have fresh water available. Use a plastic eyedropper to offer your hamster water or Pedialyte, the balanced electrolyte solution available in your grocery store's baby food area, and take it to your veterinarian. There's far more going on in your hamster's body, due to heat prostration, than you can deal with at home.

Respiratory Problems

Hamsters that have difficulty breathing may be responding to fine dust or the substrate in their caging, may have developed bacterial pneumonia, or may have a virus called Sendai. Watch for signs of labored breathing, often accompanied by discharge from the nose and eyes, loss of appetite, and weight loss. Check the caging conditions. Has any construction occurred in your house? That fine plaster dust is deadly to hamsters.

• Clean the cage, and ask a friend to take care of your pet until all the construction and painting is done. If the substrate could be the problem, change it. If you think your hamster is allergic to wood fiber or even the smell of the wood shavings/pellets, use wheat grass or hibiscus pellets.

• Has your hamster's cage bedding been dampened and you didn't catch the problem quickly? Pneumonia develops when the hamster's cage and bedding are damp, or when it is exposed to drafts. In something as small as a hamster, pneumonia causes big-time heart distress. Not only does your hamster have trouble absorbing enough oxygen across the surface of the lungs, but the heart works harder to push blood through the inflamed lungs. Heart failure or a blood clot thrown in the lungs is often the fatal result. Your hamster is probably too sick to get well on its own. Take it to your veterinarian.

• Sendai disease, caused by a virus called *Paramyxovirus,* is highly contagious and is frequently found to be widespread in hamster colonies. It also causes high mortality in mouse and rat colonies, so if you're also the owner of a fancy rat or mouse, you have double cause for concern. Half of all hamster colonies tested were positive for *Paramyxovirus*, although not every animal in those colonies was infected.

Exact diagnosis without an autopsy report can be difficult. An autopsy shows pneumonia; the lungs are filled with fluid (very typical of pneumonia), and the alveoli, the little sacs in the lungs where oxygen absorption takes place, are inflamed. No wonder it hurts to breathe when you have pneumonia! Superficially, the owner may see only a lethargic animal that seems to have trouble breathing. Alas, if your hamster has Sendai, since it's a virus, there's essentially no treatment other than keeping your hamster warm enough while his system fights the infection.

To Encourage Eating

If your hamster is ill and refuses to eat, you can try feeding vegetable baby foods with an eyedropper. Don't try to administer more than a quarter-teaspoon; remember, your hamster's stomach is small. You can also try to administer yogurt; the flavored varieties may be accepted more readily, and their higher sugar content may give your hamster a boost.

If there's any chance your hamster has Sendei, do not take it to shows or expose other hamsters to it.

Cancer

When you find a lump or an open area on your hamster's body, your first thought may be that it is cancer. If the area is actually two spots, one above each hip, relax. You've found your hamster's flank glands, a very normal part of hamster bodywork.

A hamster with a respiratory problem won't explore, but will sit, hunched over, and look distressed.

The other good news here is that the cancer rate in hamsters is among the lowest in all the pet rodents, and it is usually associated with advanced age. External tumors are usually diagnosed/recognized long before internal tumors are suspected, and the external tumors may be removed successfully. If the tumor is internal, symptoms are usually limited to weight loss and general lethargy in the hamster. One day your hamster will go to sleep and not wake up, and unless you have an autopsy done, you won't know if the cancer or old age killed him.

Gastrointestinal Problems

Enteropathies—diseases of the gut—used to be very common in pet hamsters. The diseases are spread by direct fecal-oral contact, which is kind of hard to avoid in a creature that smells everything it comes across, and fomite contamination (a fomite is anything emitted or shed by

The younger the hamster, the more serious enteritis can be.

a sick person or creature, such as mucous sprays from sneezing, saliva, feces, urine, vomit). Better husbandry and better medical treatment has turned a disease from "too bad, it's dead" to "It really can get better."

"Wet tail": Perhaps the most common disease is "wet tail." This is the bacterial disease that badly affected hamster keeping in the 1950s. "Wet tail" is used as a generic term for any type of diarrhea so acute the hamster cannot keep itself clean. Its rump is wet from the unending diarrhea; the soft, mucousy feces are on its feet, on the floor of the cage, in the bedding and if you hold it, on your hands. The odor is pungent. Not only is your hamster uncomfortable, it may be too sick to care. It is highly contagious from hamster to hamster, and particularly hard on hamsters less than 12 weeks old.

Symptoms, in addition to the stained tail and diarrhea, include lethargy, failure to eat or drink, irritability, and ruffled hair. Unless relief is quickly given, the colon may telescope into itself (intussception) or protrude out of the rectum (called a rectal prolapse). Prognosis for a young hamster is very poor even with early detection. Treatment is usually with antibiotics. Your veterinarian can identify the type of bacteria from a fecal smear, and will know which medication to prescribe.

Enterotoxemia: Another type of acute diarrhea is called antibiotic-associated enterotoxemia. Normally, your hamster's gut has a variety of microorganisms, all living more or less at peace with each other, but when that balance is altered by antibiotics, the mood "down there" can shift, with big changes in power ensuing. Pathogenic organisms bloom. At least three kinds of botulism bacteria can be found in most hamster guts, and it's not the bacteria themselves that kill the hamster, but the toxins the anaerobic bacteria secrete as part of their normal day-to-day living. Anaerobic bacteria are bacteria that live quite well without air. These are the bacteria that make a poorly sealed can of green beans swell and the ends of the can bulge out. As a group, the anaerobics are unfriendly bacteria.

Symptoms begin 6 to 48 hours after the antibiotics have been administered. They include diarrhea, swelling, and internal bleeding, The unfriendly bacteria get a toehold, so to speak, in your hamster's gut when your pet has been weakened by another disease and/or when it has been on prolonged antibiotic therapy. The normal gut flora has been thrown into imbalance by the antibiotics or a poor diet.

Talk to your veterinarian about what needs to be done. Treatment and control are through dealing with the stressing agency; for instance, is the hamster cage next to your pet skunk's bed? Move the cage to another room, high up on a table! Also, help the friendly gut bacteria become reestablished. Some people administer droplets of yogurt with an eyedropper in an effort to reestablish

Hamsters, Prions, and Ranchers

Two diseases no rancher wants to see are scrapie and mad cow disease. Both are contagious, untreatable, and ultimately fatal. Scrapie is a prion-caused fatal disease that causes abnormal rubbing or scraping behavior in sheep and goats (prions are pathogens that are simpler and smaller than viruses). Mad cow disease is characterized by progressive brain deterioration and is also caused by a prion. Hamsters are susceptible to scrapie, but may not exhibit symptoms until some time after inoculation. Why the lag? Researchers Lowenstein and Butler found that in hamsters, the incubation time—the time between infection and the actual symptom appearance—varies by the hamster species. This indicates that there is a specific gene location for susceptibility to scrapie, which means that genetic engineering could make an animal not susceptible to a prion-caused disease. This could be very good news for ranchers.

the intestinal flora; others feed their hamster the stool of another, healthy hamster, a process called transfaunation, although transfloration would seem to be more accurate.

Salmonellosis: Salmonella bacteria are found almost anywhere. Salmonella is ubiquitous in soil. Humans can get it from preparing

If a Campbell's is kept in poorly maintained communal housing before you buy it, it may "bring home" enteritis—or she may be pregnant.

eggs—the bacteria are on the outside of the eggshell. The egg is broken into a bowl or into a frying pan. Then the human, who has handled the egg, goes on to prepare the eggs for a meal and just doesn't wash his or her hands after cracking the egg. The egg is cooked and ready to eat and somehow the human touches it as it goes onto the plate. Salmonella is transferred from the human's hand to the surface of the cooked egg, which has cooled down enough so the bacteria aren't killed. The human eats the egg, and comes down with a case of salmonellosis a day or two later. Salmonella bacteria can affect hamsters as well as humans, and hamsters generally get the disease the same way we do: they eat infected food. You can avoid this by washing the fruits and vegetables you give your hamsters, the same way you would if you were going to eat them, and washing your own hands before you handle your hamster.

There may be no observable symptoms of salmonellosis. The infection overwhelms your hamster and it dies. Salmonellosis may also cause your hamster to act just a bit "off" and lose weight over a period of a few weeks. Your veterinarian will culture a stool specimen. Treatment may be with an antibiotic (see the caution on antibiotic use, page 116) or you and your veterinarian may decide that euthanization is the better answer.

Fungi and Parasites

Ringworm: We live more closely allied with fungi than many of us would like to admit. Humans get athlete's foot, which is caused by a fungus. The fungi that cause ringworm find homes in dogs, rabbits, humans, and hamsters. Hamsters that get ringworm have generally been made susceptible by damp, dirty, or stressful housing and fed inadequate diets. Symptoms of ringworm in hamsters are scaling skin, hair loss, and itching, much the same symptoms as mites. Your veterinarian will need to make the diagnosis and provide treatment.

Mites: If your hamster is losing hair, has scaling skin, or dry, scaly, scabby inflamed skin and a rough coat, and tends to scratch a lot, it may have mites. Although mites are rare in domestic hamsters, they do occur, and they are bad news. Not only does your hamster have bloodsucking tiny mites living in its skin, which is why your pet is so itchy and uncomfortable, but hamsters don't contract mites unless there's something else wrong, such as nutritional deficiencies or overbreeding. Hamsters have to be both susceptible to mites and exposed to them to contract them. Diagnosis for mites is made initially by the appearance of the hamster's skin and coat, and confirmed by a microscopic examination of a skin scraping. Mites are compact little eight-legged insect relatives, and when they are disturbed, as when taken from the soft juicy skin where they've set up housekeeping, they wave their fat stubby bristly legs around and move their mouthparts as if in silent protest. Treatment consists of a series of injections of Ivermectin, and thorough cleaning of the cage after each injection to avoid reinfestation.

Inherited Problems

Syrian hamsters are prone to a hereditary cardiomyopathy (heart failure) that produces clinical signs of congestive heart failure when the hamster is as young as six months of age. Symptoms include lethargy, labored breathing, perhaps edema or swelling, and cold extremities—pretty much the same symptoms as a human in heart failure. Diagnosis is based on clinical signs and radiographs (if you're willing to pay for these), which tells you that you have not only a very sick hamster but a very expensive one as well. Your veterinarian may want to start treatment, using much the same medications used to treat human heart failure.

When Your Hamster Gets Old

Hamsters rarely live more than two to two and a half years, and the signs of aging are pretty clear. In addition to general thinning of the hair, general slowness of reactions, lethargy, and decreased appetite, some strains of hamsters are very susceptible to liver cysts. These cysts can be very large, and cause the abdomen to bulge out. Liver failure, resulting cirrhosis, and amyloidosis (deposits of amyloids, a white protein substance, in all body organs) are common problems in hamsters over a year old.

If you are worried about your hamster being in pain as it ages, or if it is an older hamster with abdominal swelling and looks uncomfortable and isn't eating, talk to your veterinarian about euthanization. Allowing a pet to remain in pain, with no relief until it dies, seems heartless.

Hamsters in Research

The strain of Syrian hamsters that develop heart failure has been used in developing treatments for human chronic heart failure. Recently Kenneth Chien of the University of California used these hamsters to study a calcium-regulating gene and an improved method of getting that gene into the heart cells. His treatment arrested the decline for the seven months the study ran. If testing continues to show the same positive response, a version will be designed for testing in people.

Much of the research work done on hamsters involves sleep and what factors induce sleep. A lot of research deals with reproduction, and what factors influence testicular development and consequently sperm production.

But not all this reproductive fervor is concerned with hamster reproduction. Female hamster oocytes (oocytes are eggs before they are fertilized) are used to determine the viability of sperm of other animals. This is very important in cattle ranching and any other field that uses frozen sperm and assisted reproduction. Hamster ooctyes can determine the viability of frozen stallion sperm

after prolonged storage (there's big money in stallion sperm, in case you were wondering). Hamster oocytes are also used to test bovine, boar, bull, and pig sperm. The test is simple: Can the sperm wriggle into the oocytes?

Syrian hamsters—the solitary ones—have been used in obesity studies. Females kept in groups of five per cage increased body weight by 61 percent, as opposed to those housed individually, whose body weight increased 18 percent. The group-housed females had significantly larger adrenals—the glands that secrete adrenaline, the flight-or-flight hormone—than the individually housed hamsters.

Syrians also exhibit seasonal fluctuations in weight that are triggered by day length and by diet. Body weight increased when they are subjected to short days and to a high-fat diet.

Mating behavior is of particular interest in research. Female Syrian hamsters that were sexually receptive were given a choice between two males. Females invariably selected the dominant males, and spent more time in lordosis, the swaybacked "I'm receptive" pose affected by female hamsters interested in sex. It didn't matter if the females were familiar with the males or not; the winning male was always the dominant male. And the female made her selection within five minutes of meeting. Females did mate with the subordinate males, but this occurred later in the tests.

Some Syrians develop heart failure as early as six months.

Chapter Nine

Showing Your Hamster

Hamster clubs were first begun in England, to promote hamsters as a pet. They began in the 1940s (England didn't get its first hamsters until the early 1930s), not all that long after the first hamsters were smuggled into England for use as lab animals. Like dog and rabbit clubs, the members soon progressed to competitions, to showing and comparing their hamsters against those of other owners. Selective breeding was begun, to select for short noses and cobby bodies on Syrians. That's why the Syrians you see today don't look like the long-bodied creatures you may remember from the 1950s.

Today there are six hamster clubs in England, with a few more in the United States. Probably the most active society in the United States is the California Hamster Society. All of these clubs provide information on hamster keeping and hamster breeding, and most of them sponsor shows, either by themselves or as a cooperative effort with another club or society. Most of the clubs have a web page; it's hard for any organization to survive without a web presence. Most have several categories of membership, based on age and how close you might live near the club headquarters city or an affiliate club. All can arrange for international memberships

You may find other clubs; both national and international, listed on the World Wide Web, but hamster clubs tend to be a bit ephemeral. The listing may be on-line, but the club may not be active. Be a prudent purchaser. If you are interested in joining a hamster club, see if you can make contact either by phone, e-mail, or letter, with a club representative, before you send in your membership dues.

Hamster Clubs in the United States and Britain

In the United States:
California Hamster Society
32651 Dune Mear
Lake Forest, CA 92630

UK Hamster Clubs:
Clubs Affiliated to the National
    Hamster Council
The Midland Hamster Club
    Secretary—Elaine Skidmore
8, Braithwaite Drive
Kingswinford DY6 8DS
Tel: 01384 298191

The Northern Hamster Club
Secretary—Pat Richardson
7, Main Avenue
Heworth, York YO3 0RT
Tel: 01904 413426

The South of England Hamster Club
Secretary—Colin Wearn
25, Green Road
Kidlington, Oxon OX5 2EU
Tel: 01865 376686

Clubs Affiliated with the British
    Hamster Association:
(The British Hamster Association
sets show standards for the clubs
under its jurisdiction)

The Southern Hamster Club
Secretary—Wendy Barry
42 Stonebridge Drive
Frome, Somerset BA11 2TN
Tel: 01373 300766

The Hamster Society
Secretary—Grant Forrest
102/7, Whitehouse Loan
Greenhill, Edinburgh EH9 1AT
Tel: 0131 447 9045

The Heart of England Hamster Club
Secretary—Steve Roach
24 Huntercombe Lane (North)
Taplow, Maidenhead SL6 OLG
Tel. 01628 664874

The Northern Ireland Hamster Club
Secretary—Rachel Cooper
4 Rusheyhill Road Lisburn, Co.
Antrim BT28 3TD
Tel: 028 9264 8133

What Shows Are About

Hamster shows are for both the hobbyist and for the serious breeder/competitor. Although the layperson might enjoy keeping and showing hamsters, there are people who take hamster keeping and showing very seriously. Among the serious hamster people are the Avid Hamsters, who take competing as a grim, not fun, business and who will avoid competing when they don't like the judge at the show. But the majority of the hobbyists at shows are there to have fun.

Because shows exist to promote hamster keeping, hamster sales/ trades are an integral part of every show. They offer you the almost irre-sistible opportunity to buy or trade

A long-haired Syrian with a skirted coat print.

your way into new stock, a way for you to suddenly enlarge your hamster collection and shrink your wallet at the same time.

Shows may be either fun shows, or a combination of fun and conformation/color shows. The fun competition awards ribbons or prizes for the best pet, the biggest, the most spirited, the oddest color combination, the "most alike" hamster pairs. The categories are a bit quirky and apt to change from year to year. The conformation competitions recognize and award those hamsters that come closest to the British Hamster Association standards for the breed.

Pearl winter white show hamster.

Groups

Each competition is separated into Dwarf and Syrian groups; the Dwarf groups include the less frequently seen types of hamster such as the Roborovski and the Chinese rat-tailed hamsters. You can see that the Syrians still rule the roost when it comes to shows.

Shows also involve a lot of selling animals; in return for a small fee, you can sell your animals, even if you don't want to show them. This policy gives the show organizers some control over who is selling what at their show, and avoids the unpleasantness that can result when someone who only wants to get rid of his hamsters appears at the show.

Fees

Each entry requires a fee that may be less for club members, and most firmly request preregistration. You can usually preregister your ani-

mal up to the Wednesday before the Saturday show.

Qualifications

Show qualifications also include ages (typically, Syrians must be five weeks old, while Dwarfs must be four weeks old). The cooperative shows, shows that cater to mixed species such as the fancy rat/mouse and hamster shows, ask that you quarantine your show animals for a month before the show. This means that you agree to "isolate" your show animals for that time, and that you will not allow any births to occur within the quarantined group, nor will you bring any new animals into the group. Quarantine helps to avoid the spread of communicable diseases such as Sendai virus or one of the bacterial enteritis diseases. The possibility of contracting communicable disease puts fear into the heart of every hamster fancier; unless this fear is allayed, many breeders won't exhibit their

Will they be good enough? Five-week-old Syrian hamsters begin to display show qualities.

best stock at a show, which makes a show pretty pointless for the competition.

Containers

Shown animals must be in wire or plastic containers. The small to medium Pen Pals are typical show cages. Some hamster organizations have show cages you can rent for the show's duration. Each cage must contain one animal, and be stocked with clean bedding, food, and a water source. The water source can be fresh fruit such as grapes or apples; cucumbers aren't recommended because they will make your pet's fur look greasy!

Schedule

You'll be asked to check in about an hour before the show's formal opening time. This will give you enough time to pick up your paperwork at the registration table, and to have your entries checked by the attending veterinarian (this isn't always a necessity). But this sort of early checkin will also give you a chance to cruise the vendors, both for hamsters and supplies. The hamsters that are offered for sale may be placed on a separate table. Not only will there be imprinted key chains, mugs, mouse pads, tee shirts, and caging and cage accessories beyond your wildest dreams, but you'll have a chance to buy foodstuffs in bulk, often at considerable savings. And if you pick up an extra hamster here or a trio there, it's because you've gotten a terrific deal on a line you may never see anywhere else, and no one can blame you for yielding to that temptation.

How Hamsters are Grouped for Conformation Competition

Short-haired
- Self (one color)
- Standard (agouti/ticked)
- Standard (marked/banded)
- Satin (self)
- Satin (agouti/ticked/tipped)
- Satin (marked/banded)

Long-haired
- Standard (teddy)
- Standard (skirted)
- Standard (agouti)
- Satin (teddy)
- Satin (skirted)
- Satin (angora)

Rex
- Standard (rex self)
- Standard (rex agouti/ticked/tipped)
- Standard (rex marked/banded)
- Satin (rex self)
- Satin (rex agouti/ticked/tipped)
- Satin (rex marked/banded)
- Unstandardized

Dwarf hamster
Campbell's
- Standard natural
- Standard (dilute)
- Standard self
- Standard marked
- Satin natural
- Satin dilute
- Satin self
- Stain (marked)

Other Dwarf Hamsters
Winter white (standard and satin)
Roborovski (all)

Judging

Your hamster will be judged against others in its class. Judging takes only a few minutes per hamster, because judges know what they are looking for. Good behavior on the part of the hamsters is a desired quality, and many judges will penalize a biting hamster one point. Those winners are awarded ribbons and loving cups that are large enough for the hamster to use as a sleeping chamber.

In conformation shows, the BHA (British Hamster Association) standard is the best, but it isn't used for all shows. There aren't many formally trained judges who know and use the BHA standard. Training isn't easy to get in the United States; some of it is done over the Internet, from senior judges in England, and a portion of it is done in England. If you live in England, it's certainly easier to go through the training stages of book steward, pen steward, junior judge, and then senior judge.

Will this hamster win or not? Only the BHA standards can tell . . . .

Useful Addresses and Literature

Web Sites
The Complete Hamster Site
http://www.hamsters.co.uk

Hamster info
http://netvet.wustl.edu/

Organizations
California Hamster Association
32651 Dune Mear
Lake Forest, CA 92630
http://www.CHA.org

Hamsters enjoy being held and petted—but only for short periods.

American Fancy Rat and Mouse
  Association
http:www.AFRMA.org

American Hamster Association
http://AHA.org

Remember to make sure that any organization is currently active before you send in any donation or membership payment.

Books
Frisch, Otto, *Hamsters.* Hauppauge, New York: Barron's Educational Series, Inc., 1997.

Siegel, Harold, Editor, *The Hamster: Reproduction and Behavior.* New York, New York: Plenum Press, 1985.

Vanderlip, Sharon, DVM. *Dwarf Hamsters.* Hauppauge, New York: Barron's Educational Series, Inc., 1999.

Hill, Lorraine. *Hamsters A to Z.* Neptune City, New Jersey: TFH, 2001.

Walker Ernest. *Mammals of the World.* Baltimore and London: Johns Hopkins University Press, 1975.

The many faces of hamsters.

Index

The nose knows.